An Open Letter

Dear Reader,

I would like to extend a hearty welcome to you, and to make a promise. I had written and edited quite a bit before I undertook to help you write better term papers. In fact, I had and still have rather high hopes of rescuing such papers from the second-class citizenship they are often accorded in language composition courses. I realize full well that there is not much that is overtly exciting about research-oriented projects. Personally, I prefer to write short stories and poems. But through the years, I have had to turn out term papers that do not have the more accessible, warm feelings that come your way when you complete even a very dark piece of fiction. Often, I have had to grit my teeth and do my best to write something that I would not be ashamed of.

I worked my way through the cold diligence of term papers and found that the waters of objective evidence were not entirely frigid. I came to appreciate a side of myself that is possibly mature enough to find a worthwhile sense of accomplishment in writing that is at a distance from fiction and poetry. I can even trace back to term papers the development of skills that I think are definitely of value. I still prefer to write creatively, but I would be hard pressed to separate what I might have called, at one point, the grain from the chaff. They have become intertwined in my mind. And who am I to say that that is an undesirable condition?

I said that I would make you a promise, and here it is. I promise to constantly take seriously the skills in argumentation and articulation that I will talk about in this book. In my opinion, they are substantial and important to you as a human being. They will help you develop what I call "Cognitive Awareness," that is, the ability to rise above yourself and find your highest point of reasoning and morality. Often that point is distinct from your highest point of feeling. Your guts and the way you were brought up might well tell you that your own native way is the best and that anyone who does not agree with you is wrong.

Don't listen to your guts. Listen to the voice in your head. It has access to the higher harmony of Cognitive Awareness, which is you thinking about thinking. If whatever process I describe here helps you to do that, then it will have indeed been worth the months I have spent on this book. "No man is an island," John Donne said with immaculate precision. And to see the continent of the self, we have to lift ourselves by our bootstraps. That is the only way to get the vantage point we all so desperately need. So, welcome it is. I am glad to have you aboard.

Returning Later

There is a close relationship between everything discussed in this book. However, you may not, at a given moment, be interested in certain aspects of this body of information. If so, you are advised to simply skip them and return later. To facilitate this approach, there is—to some degree—an intentional, limited, built-in redundancy in the different sections. I have designed this book in such a way that the chapters are interwoven: the reader is expected to allow most of the parts to sooner or later lock themselves to one another before the beginning level of academic writing can be achieved.

Maximum Exposure and Manipulation

In my opinion, the most effective method of learning any second language is Maximum Exposure and Manipulation (MEM). That seems to be closely related to the way we acquired mastery of our first language: It must be approximated with a second. No book or method can work, however, if we simply lick our fingers after safely touching only a small part of the cake. Maximum Exposure means self-consciously immersing ourselves in the target language at every chance we get and constantly making notes in the notebook we carry around. The truly effective term in the preceding sentence is "self-conscious." I believe that all learning—especially the learning of second languages—is immeasurably more effective if we remain conscious and aware of our diligent efforts to attain that particular goal.

Consciousness of Task

I once visited a non-military American physician who was working in Vietnam during the war. The hospital was in a small, rural town and many of the expected facilities were lacking. But I saw the American doctor and his Vietnamese colleague, also a physician, as they were examining a room full of patients suffering from cataracts which covered their eyes. The doctors were going through a rigorous routine exactly as if they had been at an upscale clinic in Manhattan. They followed a protocol that involved a rather long and detailed checklist. One man would recite the items, and the other would respond in clearly audible words and very formally.

The reason for proceeding in such an overtly formal recitation of symptoms and their significance was that this was the most effective way of accomplishing their task and minimizing error. In other words, they were maximizing efficiency and effectiveness by bringing each component of the procedure to the highest consciousness--through deliberate speech. This is where focusing intently on spoken words finds a true value. No one would have criticized them if they had not recited every step, but they would have thought that they were doing their job in a second-rate manner. I do believe that they were right. Their integrity required that they do things most properly, and this required raising thoughts to consciousness through the spoken language. I learned a profound lesson that day.

I believe that all of you know exactly what I mean: it is not easy, but it is essential. Our integrity requires that we proceed in language study in the way of these men in Vietnam. Can we get by with less? We can do less and still pass the course. But this passing would be done in a second-rate manner. We are going through our experience at the university and through life only once. We will not get a second chance to correct our mistakes and half-hearted procedures. So, in my opinion, we must do it properly or not at all.

I am a hard-working creative writer and a struggling academic writer. But I can do both if given enough time and a lot of luck. I am not perfect, but I am at your service. In this book, I am offering you a seldom-encountered opportunity to learn the nitty-gritty of academic writing through research-oriented term papers. For us, "research-oriented" means "supported by objective evidence." Essentially, this is what distinguishes what we will call "term papers" from essays. A hypothesis or original idea is certainly necessary for both; but the ordered presentation of impersonal evidence that supports that hypothesis is the main ingredient of a research paper. And research done fairly and without bias is one of the main components of science. That is not to imply that essays are inferior: it is to affirm and state that they are utterly and totally different from scientific papers. Unless we realize that and act on that realization, time spent on this book

Term Papers and Academic Writing:
A Classroom Text

BECOMING A LANDMARK: The fantastically twisted trunk of this tree happens to be near the center of the remarkably beautiful, landscaped campus of New Jersey City University in Jersey City, New Jersey. It is opposite the library and near Hepburn Hall, the original Gothic-inspired building dating back to the 1930's. The unnamed tree is slowly becoming a favorite spot for students to chat, eat their lunches and sometimes even doze before a coming class

Term Papers and Academic Writing:
A Classroom Text

*For Undergraduates,
Graduate Students*

Self-Study and Use with a Teacher

by
Clyde Coreil
B.A., M.F.A., M.A., M.Ph., Ph.D.

Editor

The Journal of the Imagination in Language Learning

*Multiple Intelligences, Howard Gardner and
New Methods of Teaching College*

*The 'X' Point in Education:
Where Imagination is Lost*

Copyright © 2013 by Clyde Coreil

ISBN 978-0-7414-8184-9
Library of Congress Control Number: 2012922195

Printed in the United States of America

Published December 2012

INFINITY PUBLISHING
1094 New DeHaven Street, Suite 100
West Conshohocken, PA 19428-2713
Toll-free (877) BUY BOOK
Local Phone (610) 941-9999
Fax (610) 941-9959
Info@buybooksontheweb.com
www.buybooksontheweb.com

Dedication

This book is dedicated to the many speakers and participants in the sixteen conferences on the Imagination in Language Teaching which was founded and chaired by Dr. Clyde Coreil and Dr. Mihri Napoliello at New Jersey City University between 1991 and 2010. To these kindly educators and administrators, I say from the bottom of my heart, "Thank you. It was a marvelous ride."

Publication Information

The above conferences gave rise to the ten issues of the *Journal of the Imagination in Language Learning and Teaching*, all edited by Clyde Coreil. Every page of this considerable corpus has been copied and is available online at no charge or other requirement at <coreilimagination.com>. At least two master's theses have centered on this material, which consists of 221 theoretical and applied scholarly articles on some intersection of the imagination and language learning.

Among the stellar writers who have graced our pages are Howard Gardner, Nel Noddings, Maxine Greene, David Noonan, Diane Larsen-Freeman, Kieran Egan, James J. Asher, Earl W. Stevick, Stephen Krashen, Elliot W. Eisner, Carolyn Graham, Elana Shohamy, G. Richard Tucker, Mario Rinvolucri, Henry Widdowson, Brian Tomlinson and other eminent persons as well as teachers with a more modest publications background but also with something very well worth saying.

The contents of these ten publications are the copyrighted property of New Jersey City University and are being made available through the generosity of that institution. The website <coreilimagination.com> is under the personal ownership and control of Clyde Coreil.

An online continuation of this thrust in publication is being considered. Comments regarding this possibility are keenly sought and should be sent to Dr. Coreil at his University address (see below) or at both <ccoreil@NJCU.edu> AND at <coreil@erols.com>, his residence at 17 Fuller Place, Brooklyn, NY 11215.

Table of Contents

An Open Letter to the Reader v

Preface...1

Chapter 1: An Introduction to Preformulations 3

Chapter 2: Preformulation-Like Language Learning 12

Chapter 3: Distinguishing Features of Academic Writing 16

Chapter 4: A Metaphor of Alchemy 18

Chapter 5: Universities and the New 22

Chapter 6: Imagination and the New 25

Chapter 7: Titles, Subheads and Conclusion 27

Chapter 8: Naming the Categories 30

Chapter 9: The Necessary Hypothesis 34

Chapter 10: Plagiarism, Theft and Term Papers 37

Chapter 11: Rubrics and Evaluation 39

Chapter 12: The Thesis Statement..42

Chapter 13: Categories and Critical Thinking 45

Chapter 14: Categories and Lexical Structure 48

Chapter 15: Developing the Thesis 50

Chapter 16: Developing A Term Paper Topic 57

Chapter 17: Organization: Broad Principles..60

Chapter 18: Application of Organizational Principles 67

Chapter 19: Specific Questions to Aid in Developing a Topic 71

Chapter 20: Language...74

Chapter 21: Background 80

Chapter 22: The "Introduction" to the Term Paper..82

Chapter 23: Illustrations, Tables and Figures 85

Chapter 24: Models for Cover Sheet, Research Report 86

Chapter 25: Documentation 90

Chapter 26: Writing in the Right Voice—Formal vs. Informal........................95

Chapter 27: Evidence--In Text, Appendix, or Bibliography............................98

Chapter 28: A Sample Term Paper 100

Chapter 29: A Working Exploration of Preformulations 106

Chapter 30: Exercises in the Academic Register..117

Chapter 31: Identifying and Using Preformulations in Texts........................132

Chapter 32: Analyzing Academic Writing..134

Chapter 33: Assignments 140

Appendix 143

Bibliography 162

Figures

Figure 1:   Recursive Preformulations 8
Figure 2:   Examples of Preformulations Taught and Used....................9
Figure 3:   Repeating Detail in Conclusion 28
Figure 4:   Representation of Lexical Structure....................................48
Figure 5:   Features of Lexical Structure 49
Figure 6:   Parallel between Lexical Features and Evidence 49
Figure 7:   Lexical Source of Continuity in Paragraph Structure..........61
Figure 8:   Skeletal Outline of Academic Paper 62
Figure 9:   Example of 'Title, Author, Bio-Blurb, Abstract' 64
Figure 10: Note on Outlining 66
Figure 11: Example of Fonts for Title and Author 82
Figure 12: Forms for Copying: Cover Sheet, Research Report 87
Figure 13: Example of Bibliographic Entry 90
Figure 14: Guide to Spacing and Indentation 92
Figure 15: Practice in Academic Discourse 117
Figure 16: Examples of 'Running Notes' and Bibliographic Entry........141

is wasted. Do what I say, and there is a good chance that we will get there together. Don't do it, and you are on your own. The choice is yours to make.

Maximum Manipulation

Maximum Manipulation means that we practice forming expressions in the target language at every chance we get. All languages are treasure houses of culture with a small "c"-- living records of the uniquely different way people feel about their parents, their society, their work, their spirit, their stories, their myths, their children, their ancestors, and their great, great grandchildren whom they will probably never see. All of that is what we study when we study a second or a third language.

To understand a language, it is necessary that we focus intensely on the words and preformulations and syntax and meaning of that language. One of the most powerful tools we have to accomplish that is manipulation. We must roll each word around in our mouths as though it were a precious jewel--which it is. We must read poems written in that language. We must find objects from that culture and put them before us as we begin to write compositions and do exercises. In short, we must respect that language if we hope to move into it. If we do not use MEM, we can forget ever becoming more than tourists, possibly able to make ourselves understood but never making the big sale. If you do not approach this present book and others like it with MEM, you can forget ever writing clearly with seeming ease. You might well get a degree, but you will never speak or handle words in a manner that makes your interlocutor think that communication is little or no problem.

The Value of Predictability

Personally, I have found that students seem to prefer the predictability of an approach that follows the chapters as numbered in the book. It provides them with a valuable feeling of orientation. As a result, they seem surprisingly eager to take on difficult tasks. I have kept this principle in mind when assembling the contents of this book. Another principle I followed was the attempt to project my own, somewhat informal, personal style of teaching.

In large part, I was thinking of readers who are going through this book without a teacher. I wanted to offset the slightly dull absence of a living person in front of the classroom. No matter whether that person is interesting or not, he or she provides a center at which students can occasionally poke fun, disagree with or be surprised by. I sincerely believe that the teacher is part of a dynamic whole that is the interactive class itself. Accordingly, I strive to make limited reference to books, ideas, favorite heroes such as Nelson Mandela, Martin Luther King, Jr. and the Dalai Lama. Of course, I try to avoid becoming overly chatty, but I am aware that there is something in my role as teacher that I should not fail to play. This includes requiring students to use a certain size of font for titles and subheads in term papers, as well as requiring that they keep a record of the more interesting high-register phrases they encounter. Sometimes, it all seems to work for me. On such occasions, I thank my students for giving me an opportunity to treat them as respected colleagues.

Changing Attitudes

All too often, term papers are viewed by teachers as secondary, something the students can crank out as the pro forma product of having studied the basics of a given language. That is exactly the attitude I had for many years. Now, I am convinced that the term paper can become the central activity around which a great many other skills can be developed and brought to bear. In other words, I am trying to help rescue the term paper and turn it into a challenging learning experience.

As I made some headway in writing, I would see more and more topics that I felt I had to at least mention. The last of these was the list of 70 specific questions that might well be considerably helpful in the difficult task of finding a topic that holds particular

meaning for each student. This forms the center of "Chapter 19: Specific Questions to Aid in Development of the Topic." More precisely, the questions help you find a small area that just might make you passionate. One student once told me that she did not think that passion was a requirement. An excellent challenge! I said that, technically speaking, she was right. I added that everything in the world is so difficult that one would wisely include passion as part of the mix, part of the motivation that gets us through battle after battle with heads held high.

Now that I am done with the task of assembling a growing body of material, I believe that the book is more expansive and yet forthright than any I have seen. It is indeed tentatively that I call this work a "definitive" treatment of term papers, including preformulations and their place in Academic Writing. I might as well go one step further and recommend that this book be the primary text in writing courses, particularly when used in conjunction with *Creative Writing in College: Stories, Poems, Plays, Essays and Term Papers*. I have included term papers because they are a meaningful form of developing ideas with the rigor of the academy. I believe that they have as much right to be there as do any other kind of writing that explores the human soul. And I do believe that these two books—the one you now hold in your hands and the one on creative and applied writing--provide adequate material for a first and second course in basic writing.

A Conversation

For me, writing is most definitely an ongoing process, a conversation with myself, a comment on the fellow I was yesterday when I was working on the previous draft. When writing an essay, I keep making new beginnings and expanding paragraphs. In writing a piece for oral delivery, I keep starting over and cutting off the bottom because of time limitations. At one point, sooner or later, it is finally complete. I realize that, and I rarely add another word. For me, then, writing is an intimate part of thinking. After all this revising, I sometimes find that I am at a position that is very different from the way I was thinking when I began.

For me, writing is most definitely a way of growing and becoming more than I was. I write short stories, poems, plays, essays, letters, proposals for grants and other things, but there is never a conflict between the part of me that keeps generating language. One thing I would appreciate very much is your giving writing a chance to be for you what it is for me. Don't look forward to reaching a particular number of words and then quitting. That is like shooting yourself in both feet. If you do, you will only have to wait for them to heal before you are tempted to do it again. For me, writing is something like being in love: you are never done, nor do you want to be.

Anyway, I thought that if I dusted off some of my short stories, poems, plays and essays--if I did this and wrote more that I have been thinking of, I would have a relatively unusual collection of pieces for a college-level reader. The shortcomings of such a book would be that it does not provide an introduction to Poe, Hemingway, Steinbeck and such writers. The advantages are those that derive from choosing the kinds of work that I like and, frankly, wish to talk about with you. The creative pieces tell of a world that is full of metaphorical and real battlefields, roses, comedies and love that conquers all. I wanted to share with you what was most meaningful and passionate for me.

I did not get the idea of the second volume until I was well along with the first.. I recognize that I get a good deal of pleasure out of working in this fashion: finding order, value and direction in what might seem to be essentially waste. Of course, instructions in where to go and what to do were there all along, but I failed to see them. Now I do. Having completed work on this first volume, I will begin assembling, writing and revising the second. I hope to type the last period before the first day of summer, 2013. You are hereby invited to join me if you like.

Graduate Students

Although I have more than 40 years experience in teaching English and writing, I have never taught graduate students who will themselves teach in schools and universities. It is, therefore, not quite proper that I highly recommend that this present book be used in post-undergraduate methodology courses. However, throughout my life, I have done seemingly improper things when I was convinced that they were actually proper. And I am convinced that this book should be at least considered as one of the texts in a graduate school curriculum. I have studied in such courses and would have indeed welcomed instruction based on the kind of information you will find here.

In short, I have tried to be present in each page of both of this book. I hope that you do not get tired of me too often, and as always, I thank you for being a wonderful audience.

Sincerely,
Clyde Coreil

Preface

-1-

The Purpose of Term Papers

We should realize at every step that the research-oriented term paper is rarely an end in itself. The fundamental raison d'etre--reason for being--of the term paper is to familiarize students with the procedures and protocols of Academic Writing. The purpose in turn of Academic Writing is that it is--at the very highest level--the accepted and recognized method of exploring new areas with the intention of making and recording discoveries that are supported through the use of objective evidence. As we will point out repeatedly in this book, that is the ultimate purpose and orientation of international academia. The format we use in Academic Writing is essentially the same in all countries of the world. There are certainly minor variations, but the presentation and the principles are identical. The more we master the techniques presented in this course; the closer we will be to confidently approaching the international vehicle of academic argument and writing.

This veritable quest for new knowledge and information is what identifies us as members of the highest minded of Camelot, of virtually sacred callings that leap past the bounds of small colleges of little recognition. The size of college and its prestige in the ranks of the seemingly anointed institutions--none of that makes any difference. It is like being Christian or Jewish or Muslim or Buddhist: Is a Baptist born in Texas less Christian than the Pope of Rome? Obviously not. All academia follows the same ideals and principles of struggling to find that which is not yet known. Accordingly, it is our responsibility to learn to conduct ourselves and our research in most serious of modes. We can joke around and have fun in whatever labs we use, but we must never forget our high mission as novitiates and full members of Academia.

In writing this book, I realized as never before that clarity of presentation should be an over-riding consideration, especially for the student who reads it independently, that is, without a teacher. If writers know that there will be someone to help explain their words and thoughts, there is an almost unconscious temptation to rely on that person. If one writes for a single reader who does not have a teacher, one is far more careful about language that will ensure straightforward communication. In a sense, the obligation becomes personal.

I recall one class in my own graduate school experience when the teacher explained honestly and forthrightly that parts of the textbook we were using resisted his best efforts to understand exactly what was written. I sharply realized that the ghosts of confusion were constantly eager to nibble at and sometimes devour meaning and to trick writers into thinking that there was not a hint of the problem of comprehension. I am now certain that that problem--lack of clarity--will remain with all writers for as long as they write. The most effective weapon to fight those ghosts is, I believe, "Cognitive Awareness," a state of mind in which we are constantly ready to read and revise what we have written. Whether or not I have been successful, I have always consciously made the attempt.

1

-2-

I wrote this book out of a wish to bring together many of the insights and observations that had occurred to me in teaching college composition in general and the term paper in particular. Both of these directions involve the extensive use of preformulations, which go by many names including "chunks" and "lexical phrases." Although these structures--such as "junk food" and "get a move on"--are often mentioned, they seldom get the attention they desperately require, especially in second languages. In Chapter 1, I define them as unchanging stretches of language that recur, usually in reference to a single meaning.

Unless a student knows about preformulations, it is virtually impossible for his or her writing to be fluent. Often, that writing is difficult to understand if not incomprehensible. The student must know <u>if</u> there is a preformulation involved in a particular expression, and, if so, <u>how</u> to construct and use it. It is impossibile to talk about composition, clarity, Term Papers and Academic Writing: A Classroom Text without talking about preformulations. For this reason, the first chapter discusses the problem in some detail. In later chapters and in the Appendix, I present a great many examples and hope that the exercises help the students understand the intimate relation between preformulations and formal writing.

Of course, preformulations are very much present in general conversation. For example, I once heard a parent say when his four-year-old daughter presented him with her colored drawing: "Well, you're <u>quite the artist!</u>" Like it or not, "quite the artist" is a full-blooded preformulation. I believe that there are tens of thousands of such structures in English and every other language spoken around the globe. I also think that, in general, linguists tend to underestimate the number and importance of preformulation as a basic and ongoing principle of language and language formation.

It is my hope that after becoming familiar with this book, students will keep it for general reference. I trust that they will see that there is such a thing as an "Academic Dialect" with which they should become familiar. Chapter 31, "Identifying and Using Preformulations in Texts," will serve as a transition between this work and the language used in virtually all other college textbooks. I hope that the student will often say, "Yes. I know about this. It was explained in Coreil's book." That would make it all worthwhile.

###

Chapter 1:
An Introduction to Preformulations

NOTE: This chapter is primarily intended for graduate students and curriculum designers. Of course, freshmen and sophomores might well find it challenging reading and not out of their reach. It is an example of the "academic writing" that in many ways characterizes writing at the college level. If beginning students plow through it a couple of times, the light of understanding will likely emerge. For those who are not inclined to take up the plow just yet, I recommend that they start at "Part II: Recursive Preformulations" and that they definitely not skip "Figure 2. Examples of Preformulations Taught and Used." Last week, my current class of freshmen consciously and intentionally used preformulations in their writing. I was stunned: it was not perfect, but it was a giant leap forward.

-I-

In my opinion, there is one truly major deficiency in the manner in which language is taught and even conceived of by a great many contemporary students of linguistics. I am convinced that the neglect of what I call "preformulations" has contributed more to the lack of effectiveness in thousands of language classes than has any other single factor. I have been teaching freshman and sophomore composition for more than 40 years, and have offered 16 state and regional conferences on the subject. My experience as founder and editor of a journal on language learning and other texts is relevant. In short, I think that I am a grounded veteran, and that the opinions expressed in this text are carefully weighed. I hope that curriculum specialists, designers of courses in college composition, teachers and students--both in undergraduate and graduate schools--will take note.

The neglect of preformulated structures by theoretical linguists is regrettable, perhaps mainly because of the wide variety of opportunities for meaningful research that have gone apparently unnoticed. To say this is not to suggest that preformulations--or "chunks" or "fixed phrases" or call them what you will--are not presented as such. It is, however, to state my belief that they are considered anomalous forms and not what I think that they really are: an integral part of ongoing language formation. As a result, most classes in composition and conversation in English and any other language fail to address significantly one of the most crucial aspects of fundamental communication. In this book, I suggest a substantial correction of this most grievous situation. Because of its close connection to Term Papers and Academic Writing: A Classroom Text, I have attempted to ground in them my observations concerning preformulation.

A Definition of Preformulation

Preformulation is the process of putting together usually grammatical but often quirky strings of words, of tieing them in a fixed order to unique meanings, and of relocating these newly formed units in the lexicon. Among the simplest examples are "go to sleep" instead of "*start sleeping," "spic and span," "kick the bucket," "run away from home," "as far as," "rush to justice" and "take a taxi" instead of "*ride in a taxi." Often, the internalizing of such structures seems to occur after as few as two or three encounters with the given phrase or sentence, with the lexical items identical as is the order in which they occur. There is one exception: tense and number can be varied without damaging the preformulation--"I <u>did</u> my homework. Those issues <u>will</u> generate some heat."

Most of the preformulations we will consider are of a high and formal register. That is because it is our prime concern to make students familiar with the basic elements of an academic term paper, which is quite formal. The phenomenon of preformulation, however, is found at all registers and includes idioms, legal and technical terms, and other forms of figurative speech. Preformulations are indeed a separate body of seemingly ill-formed structures, but in their totality, they are more than that. Preformulation is a highly productive process of a constantly expanding lexicon. Once we realize that, we can begin to study this process and to make findings that would undoubtedly surprise us.

Universal Presence

Preformulation apparently occurs in all languages, which might make them more acceptable in the study of a second language. Otherwise, preformulation presents a particular difficulty for these students, many of whom have learned well the intricacies of grammar or syntax. Few of them, however, have been introduced to this manner of not only expanding the vocabulary but of knowing (1) which structures have become classically preformulated (such as "perish the thought") and (2) which can be constructed according to syntactic principles (such as the preformulation "forget about it").

It is extremely important that students as well as their teachers become aware of these basic principles of preformulation. On the one hand, it painfully adds a whole new dimension of fundamentally critical language components that must be studied and learned if fluency is to follow. But on the other, it alerts students to a process of continuing language formation which will eventually lead them to ask and answer the right questions. If they do this, they will not be constantly surprised by their teacher's marking as weak or unacceptable, structures with which students are unable to find fault. The fault is that a preformulation does exist and that this is not it.

Language itself might seem to welcome alternate means of expressing what would seem to be essentially the same concept. Personally, however, I think that there is virtually no possibility of two or more expressions being synonymous. Any variation in sentence structure inevitably accompanies a shift or change in the expression. Possibly related to this lack of synonimity is a strong inclination to bundle together particular lexical items and to shunt the whole to a new part of the lexicon or possibly of the brain.

Let us consider another very simple example: "One issue that has <u>generated some heat</u> is X." The preformulation here, "generated some heat," is used when "heat" is figurative and means "difficulty" or "anger." This expression locks out "*made some heat," "*turned on some heat," "*turned out some heat," "*caused some heat" and even the almost acceptable "*produced some heat." ***Generated some heat*** is the unit of lexical items that have been shunted to a new location. Once this occurs, there is usually no way back: one cannot unbind what has been bound.

The preformulated structure "I do" enacts the "marriage vows"--which is itself a preformulation to be preferred to "*wedding vows" or "*marriage commitments" "or "*promises made upon marriage." We have little choice but to suggest putting an asterisk before such phrases because they are simply not often--if ever--encountered in the English language as a reference to "that which is solemnly promised upon marriage."

So, although "*made some heat" might be no less syntactic than "generated some heat," it does not seem to be acceptable. This situation is found every time a choice must be made between a syntactic structure and a unique preformulated entity. One welcome "rule" is that the formula indicated by syntax is always superseded by the single preformulation--if one exists. What a student of a second language has to know is (1) Does a preformulation exist for a certain concept? and, if so, (2) What is that preformulation? There is no set of rules to follow, no way one can figure out the answer to either question. The only way one can know it is by having experience with the target language.

Chunks, Collocations, Idioms, Lexical Phrases, Etc.

What I am calling "preformulations" has certainly been recognized before in language. Words like chunks, collocations, idioms, and lexical phrases have sought to capture a feature of language formation that is essentially not rule-governed. Among the more methodical of these was work in the Functional-Notion Approach to language acquisition developed in the 20th century (Wilkins, 1976). This included an attempt to trace a top-down system of interaction between the components of preformulations. Wilkin's work was primarily concerned with the principle that specific structures are based on the needs of a given speaker to construct and communicate particular units of meaning. Such a system seems to attempt to conceive of language as essentially mathematical and logical in hierarchy between deep structure and surface structure. These concepts have themselves suffered a diminution since they were made fashionable by Chomsky (1957). Preformulation is not concerned as much with rules which are operative in the origin of such communication but with what happens after the wish to communicate is--for whatever reason--felt.

There seems to be a curious parallel between language formation and the system of patches on patches in digital programs made to solve immediate problems. (See Chapter 32 of this text.) That is to say, what seems to us to be a strangling of logic just might be an integral part of an underlying semantic reality. Possibly, the interpretation of "patches on patches" as being negative has arisen as a result of a wish to find in the essentially independent entities of communication a system of hierarchically related elements called language. Notwithstanding are the attempts to find in the speech of children clues to this supposedly vast and underlying order. For example, a child might well suggest that "ugged" is the past of the nonsense verb "to ugg." This has little or no weight in arguments concerning preformulation. If the child hears "I ogg yesterday," then he will very quickly use "ogg" as the past of "ugg." Preformulation takes precedence over rule-based regularity. At least that is my observance and assumption.

This is nothing less than burn-at-the-stake heresy to concepts rooted in the generative-- which is also mentioned less and less in linguistics recently. If we scratch a little deeper, we might find suggestions that the human mind is ultimately incapable of understanding the essential mystery of language. Of course, we have no choice but to continue looking for and sometimes even finding patterns here and there, but the Integrated Grand Scheme of Language continues to roll further and further away as we approach it--or at least seem to. At present, our explanations based on preformulations do not have to offer final solutions: their intention is primarily to make better writers of second-language students.

Canonical and Non-Canonical Identity

The preformulation of a given srtructure is possibly related to our seemingly unlimited ability to remember linguistic formulations, particularly if they are made memorable by a tag. Such a tag would consist of a seeming syntactic or semantic (grammatical or meaning) abnormality such as "take" instead of "ride in" a taxi; "do" instead of "work" one's best; and "get" instead of "arrive at" home. What emerges from this consideration of language is not so much a system of hierarchical inter-relationships, but a vast accumulation of individual, pre-formed messages, each of which is appropriate for a different specified situation. (Other aspects of this reflection are discussed in detail in pages 1 to 121 of my dissertation (Coreil, 1992).)

If we go a little further, we could suggest that a more regular aspect of grammar and semantics might be called a "canonical identity." A preformulated aspect might be called a "non-canonical identity." The non-canonical, preformulated form "Do your homework" is preferred to "*Write your homework" although homework virtually always involves writing. A somewhat more extreme example of this principle is in the preformulated phrase "Let him go" where the speaker wishes for another to be released, but there is no intention of him "going" anywhere (cf. "*allow him to go," which does indeed seem to make reference to his going somewhere).

This phenomenon of preformulation occurs throughout life. A moment's reflection will bring to mind the enormous number of words related to politics and technology that have been incorporated into English in the past fifty years. To say that the total number of preformulations in a given dialect is 40,000 is very likely to make a serious under-estimation of a lexicon that is continually marching on (Pawley, 2010).

A Radical Endorsement

One of the main goals of this book is to endorse the teaching of preformulations from the very first class in English or any other second language. Native speakers acquire their store of preformulations far more "en passant," in passing, without seeing them focused on in lessons. These structures are rarely--if ever--presented overtly as fundamentally important parts of a lexicon. They must, nevertheless, undergo internalization. If not, they will remain--as indeed they often do for Non-Natives--out of grasp. The beginning and intermediate students of English as a second language will continue to produce syntactic-like structures that deserve an asterisk. These unacceptable variants amaze the Native Speaker with just how many ways it is possible to be grammatically correct yet "unidiomatic" if not incomprehensible--all because of preformulation.

In my opinion, the reason for this deficiency in both conception and communication is the non-native failure to internalize and use the structures we are calling preformulated or "preformed." And by far the most efficient ways of doing this are (1) by consciously teaching them one by one, and (2) by encountering them repeatedly in readings that are carefully selected and constructed. That is precisely what I am suggesting, and this is where the designers of language curricula do indeed come in. They are in an excellent position to influence attitudes toward the shaping of language, and to coordinating the conscious and sub-conscious encountering of individual components of the vast store of preformulations. There are a few regularities involved--such as "getting in" a small vehicle and "getting on" a large vehicle"--but most preformulations are acquired individually.

Correcting a Situation

One way to begin correcting this situation is by teaching preformulations as consistently and as overtly as other items in the lexicon. Of course, what we need is a "Dictionary of Preformulations." Not having that, we can at least begin assembling and developing lists of such structures. I have done this with some 100 preformulations, which I taught to advanced ESL students (See Chapter 29: A Working Exploration of Preformulations). I asked students to intentionally and consciously use these structures in summarizing or commenting on short stories and poems we had read in class. This was, of course, sometimes awkward and imperfect, but I found that it could be done: please see the examples presented at the end of the current chapter.

Chapter 30: Exercises in the Academic Register attempts to offer practice in blending the fully formed preformulations with other aspects of the style of the formal manner of writing and speaking that we would likely identify as "Academic Discourse." Although it is imperative that advanced graduate students master this mode of speech, it is seldom if ever overtly addressed in a course. Chapters 29 and 30 barely scratch the surface in the conscious analysis and instruction in this specialized and high register.

Variations of these exercises could be developed and taught from the first class on. I believe that this direct way of exposing students to a great number of preformulations would be effective. To use the more natural method of "chance encounter" would quite likely be better--if a large number of years and situations were available. Obviously, such is not the case. On the other hand, the winds are with us in that our capacity for remembering exact phrases and short sentences is virtually unlimited. For example, some individuals can cite verse and chapter of the entire Bible and similar documents.

"Gim-me uh Bud"

We might mention here that preformulations are by no means limited to the higher registers. "Gim-me uh Bud" is far more effective in the rough-and-tumble world of a working-class bar than the more delicate, "I would like to have a Budweiser, please." The latter sentence seems considerably more proper but also far more dangerous in inviting ridicule and worse. Obviously, what I am suggesting would require a revamping of much of an entire curriculum. I gulp when I say that, but one must call a spade, a spade. In my opinion, the sooner we begin, the sooner we will finish.

-II-

Recursive Preformulation

As a result of preformulation, one concept is tied to one surface structure, which in turn wraps its tentacles around that single concept. In other words, the concept and the preformulated expression are in a virtually unbreakable, mutual lock. Unless a student is aware of the specific double-lock involved, he or she cannot properly conceive of and express a given idea. Instead of "fast and furious," the student will say "*quick and furious." Instead of "get the hang of it," the student might say "*learn the hang of it." As we get into the more abstract regions of physics and mathematics, we find that a linguistic structure is bound to a single concept such as "Absolute Elsewhere."

A slightly more complex structure is fashioned by putting together two or more of these strings in a "recursive preformulation." To consider a straightforward example, see Figure 1. It is to be noted that "have played" is a verb form, but that verb forms—or any kind of forms—can also be preformulations: this is admittedly somewhat speculative but interesting.

****

Figure 1. Recursive Preformulations: Individual preformulations can be combined to make other preformulations. For example:

> A. __X__   is thought to   __V__. (The words "is thought to" constitutes a
>   preformulation.)
> B. __X__   has played a major role in   __Y__. (Preformulations are underlined.)
>
> C. __X__   is thought to have played a major role in   __Y__. ("A" and "B" are
>   combined.)
> D. John's anger is thought to have played a major role in his getting fired.

In sentence "D," *John's anger* replaces "X" and *his getting fired* replaces "Y." The resulting sentence is an example of multiple recursive preformulations: A, B, C. and D.

****

Shunting

Syntax is that property of language by which precisely different relationships between entities, time, location, cause, effect, and agent are conceived and expressed. Our understanding of these factors has become well developed in the past 100 years. Our understanding of the phenomenon of preformulation, on the other hand, has made little if any progress, possibly because of its seeming shallowness and the resulting lack of direction that serious research might pursue. This is unfortunate for the very process of preformulation remains virtually undiscovered. For example, what is involved in the shunting or movement of these structures to a probable different part of the lexicon or brain?

Possibly, there is no movement but rather a cocoon-like neuronic enwrapment of components such as "is thought to." Something happens to the unit of words that is shunted: for example, those units seem to be remembered better than the component words themselves. Probably, the association of "cocoons" and "neuronic enwrapments" is excessively fanciful. Yet, for some reason, the units certainly seem to behave differently from their components. If something is needed to make this process more interesting to theoretical linguists, I think that the shunting might be a proper and needed initial step.

-III-

I have seen first-hand the dramatic effect that the overt, intentional and specific teaching of preformulations can have in language class, particularly in conceiving and effectively expressing concepts. I present evidence of this in two lists of 100 such structures in chapters 29 and 30 (See Figure 2). In the Appendix to this text, I also present a copy of my essay entitled "Preformulations: A Needed Sea Change in Language Instruction" which appeared in *The 'X' Point in Education: Where the Imagination is Lost* (2011). In the latter piece, I attempt to present a number of substantial and wide-ranging reasons for considering preformulations as structures of the first importance in language. My 1992 dissertation in linguistics at the Graduate Center of the City University of New York --*Fusion in Language: A Case for Supralexical Units*--also deals fundamentally with this notion. These writings constitute external, objective evidence which support my basic hypothesis: That preformulations should be consciously fore-fronted as a primary element in all foreign and second language lessons.

I delay presentation of these extensive exercises and the essay so as not to overwhelm the other parts of this text, parts dealing with a formal approach to the writing of academic term papers at the level of the college freshman. The three--preformulations, term papers and academic discourse--are closely intertwined and offer an excellent opportunity to present an integrated perspective. Hopefully, the abbreviated presentation in Figure 2 immediately below will tend to make students aware of the phenomenon of preformulation and of sensitizing their perceptive faculties accordingly. (This information is found again in the Appendix: for the sake of clarity, I present it twice.)

###

****

Figure 2. Example of Preformulations Taught and Used: *The Imagination of Daedalus* and *Parents and Asperger's Syndrome* contain examples of the use of preformulations in academic writing.

  A. List of high-register preformulations from Academic Discourse. Note that in this list, "X", "Y" and "Z" are noun positions; "V" is a verb; "C" is a clause.

1. Mention should also be made of __X__ .
2. __X__ has to do with __Y__ .
3. Had it not been for __X__ , __Y__ would have __V__ .
4. In this paper, it is my goal to __V__ .
5. I have tried here to show that __C__ .
6. __X__ is a key element in __Y__ .
7. __X__ is a legitimate field of study.
8. __X__ has more in common with __Y__ than with __Z__ .
9. This will involve at least a cursory study of __X__ .
10. __X__ can also decrease efficiency.

  B. The following is a writing exercise aimed at having students internalize the above structures (1-10). Students were asked to write a coherent comment on the account of Daedalus and Icarus as presented in the non-ESL textbook *Retellings: A Thematic Anthology* published by McGraw-Hill Company in New York. In order to provide a model, I executed this assignment:

The Imagination of Daedalus
by Clyde Coreil

Icarus fell into the sea, not because of tension between him and his father, Daedalus, but because of a strong wish to explore the world on his own, even if it meant ignoring his father's cautious advice. Pride of his new skill in flying **was a key element in** the boy's tragic accident. Often, youth **has to do with** assertion. That is as true today as it was in ancient Greece. Indeed, Icarus **had more in common with** a young teenager of 2010 **than with** a man of 45, either in Greece or Jersey City. **In this paper, it is my goal to** point out that neither Icarus nor his father was at fault. **This will involve at least a cursory consideration of** the reason Daedalus encouraged his son to fly. **Had it not been for** Minos, who was holding them prisoner on the island of Crete, the father **would not have** suggested the sky as a way out.

Today, aeronautics **is a legitimate field of study**. In Ancient Greece, it was against "the laws of nature." Nevertheless, Daedalus used his imagination to design and construct wings, not only for himself but also for Icarus. **Mention should also be made of** the fact that he wept out of deep concern for the danger he was putting his son in. Yet sadness and worry **can decrease efficiency**, so Daedalus concentrated on his task. When the wings were complete, he cautioned his son to be careful and not go too low or too high.

I have tried here to show that although he was imaginative and even artistic, Daedalus was also a loving father. It is ironic that although his invention of human wings was successful, it was this same genius that proved to be the occasion of his profound loss. Leaving his island prison, he found another in his son's tomb.

###

I was ready for Icarian disaster when I asked the students to use the preformulations from a second short list. But lo and behold, I got some decidedly decent pieces of writing from them. Below is one student's execution of a similar list of ten advanced preformulations, which are again in boldface.

Parents and Asperger's Syndrome
by Sejal Shah

This finding suggests that not only do children with Asperger's Syndrome have a hard time dealing with it, **but** parents do too. **Little is yet known about how or why** the children became sick from Asperger's Syndrome. **Children that were said to be** autistic behaved differently. Behavior **was poised to play a major role in determining** if something was wrong with a child. Parents that have children with Asperger's Syndrome have different problems to worry about as opposed to those who have children that are normal. More than anything parents have to accept their children first and teach those children how to accept that they have Asperger's Syndrome. Parents **should lay to rest the fears of** children having Asperger's Syntrome. If parents don't accept it, then children will have a hard time coping with themselves and it will be harder for them to live their life as normal as they can.

Having Asperger's Syndrome **is thought** to make you behave differently from others, but it doesn't stop you from being human beings. **It does not follow, therefore, that** they aren't capable of living a normal life, because they are; and doing things the rest of the kids are doing. **To say this is not to deny that** it can affect the siblings of those with the disorder. **It is also worth mentioning that** you have to just have patience and train them well and make them familier to the world, which will show them that it is okay to have Asperger's Syndrome. They might not be able to control their emotions and such things, but that is what makes those kids special. **It is important to make clear that** they also have the ability to do things individually and that's how it can be proven wrong to those people that believe Aspergers Syndrome is a mental disorder. **A definitive history of** Asperger's Syndrome **remains to be** written.

****

Chapter 2:
Preformulation-Like Language Learning

It does seem to be the case that memorizing a particular preformulation is a rather extreme version of one of the central processes in learning a language. Although syntax is an important part of constructing a satisfactory sentence, it is limited in that language cannot be generated from a set of syntactic rules alone. Once we have the concepts in mind, we usually arrange the components of the lexicon in syntactic order. However, knowing which words are required to convey the concept is essential: we must know what to input into the syntactic network.

On the next level up, we must know how to articulate the concepts that we are working with, and how to filter out the articulations that do not convey those target concepts. Here the analogy to preformulations is quite useful. The possible concept-articulations that we are <u>not</u> working with are virtually limitless in number. It seems far more likely that we learn the single effective articulation and automatically reject the others, no matter how pristine their syntax appears to be. It is highly relevant that we become aware of each of the good ones, of each articulation that will do what we want it to. For example, read the following sentence carefully:

"I want to leave a flying airplane by stepping out of the door and making the parachute that is attached to my back unfold at the pulling of my ripcord."

There is no mistake in syntax or grammar in the above sentence. However, there is something very awkward about that sentence. It begins to approach the incomprehensible. If I say the following sentence, I will have approached but not quite reached the acceptable:

"I want to jump with the parachute."

If I make a couple of additional minor changes, my sentence becomes satisfactory:

"I want to make a parachute jump."

The correct, fully acceptable, preformulation-like expression is "to make a parachute jump."

Whether or not we want to classify that expression as a preformulation is not very important to the non-linguist language learner. What is important is being aware that a given language has chosen to require a given formulation in this instance. Our speech will be awkward—and possibly incomprehensible--if we do not know (1) that a preformulation-like expression is required and (2) how that notion is put together in words. Exactly the same situation exists for a huge number of concepts. Whether we consciously learn a given expression or acquire it more haphazardly by chance, we must become able to unconsciously form our sentence with "make a parachute jump" and not "*jump with the parachute." This is an enormously important principle in learning a second language.

Apparently, one of the most effective ways of learning a second language is by what I call "Maximum Exposure and Manipulation" (MEM)—reading, listening, writing, making mistakes that are corrected by someone. This "MEMorization Method" must occur with a great many articulations. I have formalized this principle in the following exercise. Please read a passage in any textbook or novel that is written by a native speaker. Then isolate a single stretch of two to six words of a sentence that you wish to learn. Write that part on a given line. Finally, construct an original sentence that includes the target..

****

Exercise in Constructing Sentences from Targets: Please read the following passage and underline each expression you are isolating. Then, write a complete sentence that includes the isolated or "targeted" segment of the sentence. (In the passage below, I have identified and underlined the targeted segment.)

<u>To summarize, it is reasonable to conclude that</u> the experience of creating a work of art was a positive one for these secondary students of French. Almost all of them <u>responded positively</u> to the opportunity to create their own artwork: they <u>devoted substantial time and effort</u> to the artistic process, and created truly unique and personal images in Impressionist-inspired style. Moreover, the student's positive response to the creation of artworks <u>had implications for</u> the classroom, which became a community of artists <u>sharing ideas</u> and support. Finally, this <u>positive attitudecarried over into</u> the students' written self-expressions in French. <u>In their essays,</u> students <u>not only</u> communicated effectively using new vocabulary, they also went beyond description to <u>provide interesting insights</u> into their artwork.

The Journal of the Imagination in Language Learning, Volume 2, p. 82.

Instructions: On line "A," please copy the target you have underlined in a passage. On line "B," please construct an original sentence that includes the target.

Example: 100-A. <u>to summarize</u>
100-B. <u>To summarize, Brazilians set a good example for enjoying life._____</u>

1-A. <u>it is reasonable to conclude that</u>_____

1-B. _____

_____

2-A. <u>responded positively</u>_____

2-B. _____

_____

3-A. <u>devoted substantial time and energy</u>_____

3-B. _____

_____

4-A. had implications for_____

4-B. _____

_____

5-A. sharing ideas_____

5-B. _____

_____

6-A. positive attitude_____

6-B. _____

_____

7-A. carried over into_____

7-B. _____

_____

8-A. in their essays_____

8-B. _____

_____

9-A. not only_____

9-B._____

_____

10-A. provide interesting insights_____

10-B. _____

_____

****

(You are encouraged to make copies of the following page for practice.)

Constructing Sentences
From Preformed Targets

Instructions: On line "A," please copy the target you have underlined in a passage. On line "B," please construct an original sentence that includes the target.

Example: 100-A. it is reasonable to conclude that_____

100-B. He said <u>it was reasonable to conclude that</u> class will not be cancelled.

1-A. _____

1-B. _____

_____

2-A _____

2-B. _____

_____

3-A. _____

3-B. _____

_____

4-A. _____

4-B. _____

5-A. _____

5-B. _____

6-A. _____

6-B. _____

7-A. _____

7-B. _____

8-A. _____

8-B. _____

9-A. _____

9-B. _____

10-A. _____

10-B. _____

****

Chapter 3:
Distinguishing Features of Academic Writing

In its broadest meaning, a term paper is a piece of writing by a student over the course of an entire semester or "term." We will limit the comments and instructions below to one particular type of term paper which might be called "argumentative" or "persuasive." In this kind of term paper, it the main intention is to convince the reader that the writer at least has a body of evidence that is strong if not compelling. This implies that some readers will disagree and have to be convinced that the author has presented worthwhile evidence in a professional manner.

Interestingly enough, this inclination of some readers to disagree is a sign that our topic is appropriate. This simple principle also serves to reinforce an important feature of academic research papers: they do not affirm popularly held beliefs. Following are extreme examples of such terrible beliefs: "Most mothers love their children," "Junk food is usually unhealthy," "Lazy students often fail to succeed," and "Bacteria can cause disease." No one would begin to challenge you about these topics. Nor would anyone be interested, including members of the college community. Virtually everyone assumes that they are true.

If, however, you can provide evidence to reverse these, then you have a topic that might be worth pursuing. For example: "Junk Food: Sometimes a Healthy Alternative." Aha! Here is a paper that does something new: it says that junk food is not always "junk." The reader will probably disagree at first, but he or she would have difficulty resisting the urge to see what you have to say. Of course, you have to cite valid evidence that what has been improperly classified as junk food can be indeed healthy.

If you cannot do that, you have tricked the reader who will throw this paper into the trash basket or maybe even give the paper a grade of "F". In essence, you would have lured him or her with a misleading thesis statement. In chapters 9, 12 and 15, we discuss the idea and the articulation of the all-important thesis statement, and we go into detail about six characteristics on a checklist. I think you will also find "Remarks on the Thesis" (in Chapter 15) to be important and easy to understand.

Commitment and Passion

Behind most academic writing, you will find a highly committed and even passionate belief in the possibility that the writer is dealing with a new idea. That commitment and enthusiasm is excellent. However, that writer must be careful to guard his or her formal objectivity and remain emotionally neutral in the presentation of the argument. It is a most serious error to use words like "fantastic," "wonderful," and "marvellous" in the presentation of evidence. Our stance must be unemotional, we must not say more than our supports warrant. To sum up, enthusiasm is truly to be desired; yet we must not betray that enthusiasm anywhere in the term paper.

Towards a Change in Thinking

The second aspect of the paper we will describe is concerned with establishing or changing the way a given topic is thought about at the present time. Accordingly, academic papers are not addressed to only one reader: they must provide evidence that will be accepted by many readers. Neither are you allowed to use any of the personal pronouns except "we," and that is the "editorial we" and not a group of people. This "editorial we" is used when you are telling your reader about attitudes and procedures that will be pursued in the paper you are writing. Do not use "I, you, he, she, they or them." Be very careful not to use "you" as in "You will understand as more and more topics are introduced." On the other hand, the Passive Voice is very well accepted in Academic Writing. Passive = "be + past participle" as in "Chemistry <u>will be studied</u> by the students next year."

The third aspect is that the writer uses relevant, objective evidence to support his thesis. The fourth is that he or she will not suppress evidence that does not support it. Generally, evidence that seems to support the current or old state of an idea belongs in the discussion of "Background." Usually, that is the place in the term paper to mention some small part of the evidence that did not support the new idea. If a lot of your evidence does indeed support the existing idea and not your new idea, you will have no choice but to alter that idea or change the topic completely.

Conclusion

The term paper that we will describe is oriented around the new. Sometimes, the new element is a new finding or discovery that is quickly gaining recognition. Sometimes, the paper itself will be the vehicle of the discovery and presentation of the new. An example of this is your having assembled objective evidence that strongly suggests a different interpretation of known relationships.

What is always very true about academic term papers is that they demand the close, almost passionate participation of you, the writer. It is essential that you become deeply involved in convincing the doubters with compelling evidence presented calmly that you are right. It is far from enough for you to check the internet a couple of times and then begin writing the final version of your term paper. However, if you try to do that, rest assured that you will probably have another opportunity of studying with me again next semester. More seriously, you have a difficult job ahead of you. If you accept that and put forth your very best effort, you will be able to do it. If I see that you are working very hard, your success or failure will be mine as well. If you do not commit yourself, your failure is your own.

###

Chapter 4:
A Metaphor of Alchemy

Often, teachers have general reading and writing as their main topics in a freshman composition course. They require a term paper, mainly as evidence that their instruction has been effective. That is indeed the way I used to approach this course. This semester, however, I am going to reverse the order of attack. Our main subject will be the development and writing of a term paper. Because we have only 14 weeks to hone this relatively new skill, I am going to specify one particular type of development, although I am very much aware that many other models could quite successfully be followed. My argument is the following: if we were to consider even a few of the possible variations, the end of the term would be upon us, and we would not have made much progress. If we adhere to a single model, I think that that model will come under your understanding and control.

Regardless of whether I am right or wrong, that is what we will do. If other teachers use this book, they are very welcome to specify changes. If they do, it will be because they are different individuals, and their teaching will always tend to reflect their individuality. If we were to attempt to all do the same thing at the same time and in the same manner, we would be vastly underestimating the truly positive aspects of individuality and the imagination.

All too often, classes are seen as groups of students waiting to be given a certain number of specified cookies that are initially contained in a large box carried by the teacher. At the end of the semester, the teacher counts the number of cookies held up by each student, and grades would be assigned accordingly. We can call that method "The Counted-Cookie Model." There is little or no variation required or in fact taken into account. The effectiveness of the teacher is supposedly completely under control and can be very closely measured. If 150 elements--such as Run-On Sentence, Capitalization, Pagination, Presence of Thesis Statement--are specified, then the student and teacher know how the performance of both is determined. All is circumscribed by someone in a higher office who indicates the discrete elements that must be taught by the teacher and learned by the student. This attitude becomes even more limiting and self-defeating when it becomes part of a protocol of judgment by agencies analogous to the "higher office."

A Gross and Offensive Underestimation

This method is good in that at least a bare minimum of learning will probably occur in the classroom. It is, however, seriously deficient in that it assumes that the teacher knows everything that the student will learn in the course. This is a gross underestimation of the very process of education itself, an opinion with which Socrates would undoubtedly have been in agreement. The student's natural inquisitiveness and interest will very likely lead him or her to explore ideas that sometimes have not even been overtly discussed in class. This is a situation devoutly to be wished for. The teacher of such a student should feel justified pride in having helped to provide the space and atmosphere for this to occur. More precisely, the teacher will have helped provide for an invaluable imaginative interaction between the student and the subject being studied.

The "Counted-Cookie Model" says nothing about establishing an activated imagination deep within the student, which some see as a necessary condition for the dynamic and often profound mental activity of <u>both</u> the teacher and the student. The student needs the encouragement and reassurance of the teacher in pursuing relationships between, say, the point at which too much sports is too much; the place of language in regard to identity and self-confidence; the concept of honor in the school. And the teacher needs support in order to talk seriously about these most meaningful values.

A slight extension of the principle holds that education is always a two-way process in which the teacher often learns more than the student. In other words, "The Counted-Cookie Model" makes no provision for the growth and development of the teacher. It conceives of education as the static distribution of a fixed number of Cookies. The lack of mutual, teacher-student support means that little or no attention is given to the most precious gift that the teacher has to offer--a confident belief that a bright spirit will open its wings and embrace the teacher and his or her students. If that does happen, the teacher and the students will have entered a relationship in which teachers can learn from students, and students can learn from teachers. The material that can be taught and learned by each group is, of course, quite different. But it is always substantive and it is always possible.

This is not some sort of tattered remnant of a Maoist-like Cultural Revolution or an avant garde, Utopian classroom, but rather a very old-fashioned situation in which mutual respect is a prime and commonly found element. If it happened routinely in the past, why is that now, mutual respect between teacher and student is often missing. Ask any teacher if this is true, and you will understand my position. That is the exciting part of teaching: to turn a blind eye to it is to shoot oneself in both feet.

A Highly Relevant Metaphor

Once I described such relationships metaphorically in a piece called "The Alchemist's Swan" (Coreil, 2007). I copy the main part of that description and place it below. I ask that you read it carefully. If you do not understand it, read it again. If again, you don't understand it, then that is still wonderful because then we will have a very interesting something to talk about. You might ask, "Why are we talking about this now?" There are two reasons. First, because sincere commitment and involvement is essential to writing an effective term paper. It is very difficult to write convincingly about something we do not feel honestly involved in. I hope that your attitude toward your term paper is not at all like the attitude of the rough man in the crowd you will read about below.

The second reason is so that you might realize the power of all metaphor, which is related to lexical structure we will read about in Chapter 14. Briefly, metaphor is the use of one set of references--such as those associated with "fishing"--in speaking of another topic--such as "romance." Fishing reminds us of romance in that the fisherman never knows if his bait will attract the kind of fish that he is after. Can you think of other ways in which the two activities have features in common? It is part of the powerful muscle of language, and you should be aware of it and not be afraid to use it in essays and other imaginative writing. We are now taking a short break from straight academic writing.

The Alchemist's Swan
Part 2: The Metaphor
by Clyde Coreil

As the drape covering the large statue at its exhibition is ready to be lifted by a rope and pulley, everyone is filled with apprehension. There is a long pause, then up the cover climbs very slowly. Finally revealed in their entirety are two highly polished golden ovals, each five feet in length. They are both standing on end. There is a murmur here and there, but generally everyone is waiting, sitting on the edge of their seats. Then the magic begins. The ceiling of the Secret Transformational Laboratory (STL) is high, and the air is amazingly fresh despite its thick aroma of magic, potent herbs and boiling flasks. Enter "The Alchemist" in gorgeous, deep purple robes and a long and a long and floppy cloth hat that Oscar Wilde would have behaved himself for. The surface of the fabric ambiguously played with the image of a night sky in the aboriginal Rockies. The Divine Creator had outdone himself on that one. The stars filled the black with distant, beautiful chords of heavenly subtlety.

"Each oval represents a concept," the aging Alchemist said, and produced an object covered in a deep red cloth. There seemed to be movement under the cloth, but no one could be sure. He put the object next to one of the ovals, and the object and the oval seemed to interact. At times the motion was incredibly fast; at other times, everything seemed perfectly still. Finally, the Alchemist lifted the red cloth and there was a round opening in the oval. He reached inside and took out two sparkling gems. The audience caught its breath! Then, before they could say anything, he put the cloth and the object next to the other oval. The action was the same. He removed three gems and placed them beside the other two on the table before him. The Alchemist waved his wand over the concepts, and the openings were instantly closed. His old and wrinkled hands took up the gems and molded and spun them into a beautiful swan which looked at the audience demurely and then paddled away effortlessly.

"I have given you," the Alchemist said and paused to make certain that the attention of everyone in the room was focused on him as though he were the hard-burning fire that could answer their most precious questions. "I have given you the metaphor of the imagination. It is the single secret I hold most dear in my heart. Study it and tell your children and close friends that, next to love, tolerance, and true humility, it is the most precious and meaningful of lessons they will ever encounter. It will guide them to the most distant stars and through the blackness of the deepest ocean. The only thing that can ever stop its magical transformations is the loss of confidence. The imagination is the key to all of creation: all it asks is that you never let its glow be hidden. If you do, you will doubt that it was ever anything but the idle fantasy of a lazy child. He turned and the room had become a bower, and he was walking very near the edge of the water where the seemingly translucent bird was floating gracefully. He reached into his pocket and took out an assortment of nuts and grain that the swan began to eat ravenously.

Then a rough man in the back of the room said, "Hey! Is that all? The guy who sold me the ticket said that a divine secret would be revealed in here. So I gives him a dollar and comes inside and all that I hear is this yakking about a big goose." Immediately, he saw that the magnificent swan had turned into a goose, honking angrily like one of those old-fashioned brass horns that are attached to black rubber bulbs. For the man who had spoken out, The Alchemist turned into a small and ugly creature whose face was full of displeasure and even hate. He was a walking bomb, waiting for the smallest reason to explode into the foul stink of a dozen really rotten eggs. Across the room, there were small poppings as the swan and The Alchemist became the honker around whose neck was a noose and a thick cord held by the nasty guy who suddenly stopped. The goose squawked and wanted to get away, but every time he did, the cord became tighter.

The owner of the goose with dirty feathers yanked his bird and came back to the center of the room. He looked at each man, woman and child in the crowded enclosure which had begun to smell of tobacco, unflushed toilets, overflowing garbage cans and and everything else that made one choke and threaten to vomit.

"Hah!" the man said and squeezed the head of the goose which had become an old and cracked rubber duck. "Hear that?" He squeezed again and the duck responded with a wheezing, whistling sound. "That stinking old bum had almost bamboozled you again. The Glorious Imagination," he said, rolling his protruding eyes skyward and mocking. "What a crock. And you'd a sworn that he was giving you a secret he got from his own private angel." The man then leaned into the crowd and whispered, and everyone told everyone else to "Shut up!"

The bum who had complained waited until the hall was as quiet as a mouse. "He's looney, he is. Crazy as the day is long. Don't you go believing all that malarkey about the imagination. That'll get you into big trouble. Things is what you see, not some fairy tale about an old woman who lived in a shoe, or some little boy who blew a flute and some sort of genie whooshed out." He stopped and looked into each eye. Then all at once, he shouted and the little children shouted and started to cry: "If you think you got it bad in your stinking lives now, you just go along and believe all that nonsense. The only thing he ever cracked with his 'magic wand' was a peanut and maybe the head of an old lady whose purse had caught his eye.

A Modest Credo

So there you have it. And in metaphor in the form of an old-fashioned tale to boot! Why didn't I just come right out and say that the loss of confidence in the imagination is among the most treacherous obstacles in the path to a fuller and fuller realization of what the human mind can hold? I do believe that. I also believe that for some dark reason, we keep on calling, not for the magical swan but for the cracked and wheezing rubber duck which represents propriety and prestige. The swan, on the other hand, represents the existential magic of becoming what we and the things around us are not. A cosmos of possibilities is ours for the asking.

In each of our minds, there are countless shining ovals and the red cloth of the imagination is always only a wish away. But again and again, we turn from the swan and the magnificent possibilities and go with the rubber duck of propriety and prestige. So that, if we want the swan, we must remain vigilant lest we lose faith and thereby let ourselves be fooled into the tragic belief that the imagination is nothing but a "big goose." I believe that metaphor is the home of the imagination. And that the human capacity to perceive the truth of things as they are is severely limited. And that the imagination is the one divine gift that can light our night.

###

Chapter 5:
Universities and the New

Virtually all universities have, among their primary goals, teaching and research--often a combination of the two. The teaching is not of all knowledge. Astrology, shoe repair, the manufacture of musical instruments, the design and making of mechanical hearts--such areas are usually outside the purview of the university and are more related to trade and commerce. Physics, city planning, literature, the history of culture, mathematics, philosophy--these fields are well represented on college campuses around the world. It is possible to get through many of these classes by occasionally showing up for class, presenting fallacious excuses, and weaving most insubstantial answers to questions on exams. Those three acts of chicanery will often get you out of that particular class with a "C-" or a "D." You will have wasted a lot of money and even more precious time. The chunk of years and your almost blessed status as a "college student" will not be recoverable.

The Bottom Line: Becoming

One unifying goal of all legitimate universities everywhere is the discovery of what is unknown based on an understanding of what is known. Often discovering what is new involves revising what was thought to be known and established. Sometimes, establishing an academic response to something not known at the present will qualify as the legitimate element. Regardless, it is discovering the new that is always near the heart of the university. One reason why we learn about current ideas is so that we will understand the process of changing them.

What I am about to tell you now is something that no one told me when I was an undergraduate, but it is such a fundamental, underlying point on which most undergraduate and graduate studies are built that you must be informed. It is simply the fact that is no great body of information that can be consulted to determine what is the final thought about anything in academia, no matter how basic. The universities in all parts of the globe--academia, in short--are constantly in the process of discovering unknown things or changing what was thought to be known. The university as stone building must be replaced by the university as a whirling flux of changing elements.

Academia is an ideal, an abstract dream, a gigantic machine, parts of which are located wherever seekers of true knowledge are willing to brave the establishment in order to get a fair hearing. As a member of the university community, you share a pursuit that is common to the whole world. Who cares about the prestige and status of your particular institution? The things you do within these walls are exactly what your young and old colleagues in every country are doing.

If you are successful here, your will be successful everywhere men and women are drawing breath. In a very real sense, academia is an elevated pursuit of an elusive truth that is constantly being changed in detail. That is what it is, no matter how little some of us faculty or the administrators view it in a very different light as a corporation, the bottom line of which is profit. The president of this university has a background in "university advancement." This is an evolving part that used to be associated with public relations and fund raising. This is very important to the continued existence of our university, especially since the state government has been decreasing its contribution to our budget. The difference has been partially made up by increases in tuition and related fees. In an apparent attempt to remain alive, different universities in this country have begun increasing the ancillary services such as physical fitness centers.

Although these models have become more and more popular, they are essentially aspects of models for administrators. The nerve center of the university remains the students and faculty and their joint pursuit of new information and theories. We must guard the almost sacred honor of our Camelot, and view our pursuit of truth as the highest part of ourselves. That model is, in my opinion, far more in touch with the real world than some for-profit institutions that are interested mainly in the enterprise called "university" as the source for more and more income and little else.

In my opinion, it is critical that you students and we faculty be aware of the ideals that have sustained us for centuries. Although the university might be considered as a business whose bottom line is profit, it is far more than that. It is the eyes and ears by which society comes to terms with the relationship between the past and the future. Even businesses cannot be concerned only with profit and loss. If we consider ourselves as interested only in money, then we are lost. The master said, "I have a dream" and was taken into the hearts of virtually everyone on the face of the globe. If he had said, "I have a corporation," none of us would even know who Martin Luther King, Jr. was.

When you were accepted as a student here, you were automatically given membership in a brotherhood that far exceeds the social. It is a fraternity and sorority that aims at exploring the known world in hopes that you as an individual will be able to exercise your divine right and duty to uncover new meaning. The fundamental relationship that exists between human beings and reality is one of change and discovery and existentially becoming what we were not before. The university is different from every known business where material gain is the bottom line. The bottom line here is becoming. The thrust to change based on evidence is what we are about. Forget that and you will have surrendered your identity.

The Search for Knowledge

Undergraduate classes are often concerned with imparting knowledge about the existing state of some idea, process or physical entity. As the student advances to the higher levels of study in graduate schools, university education becomes centered more around expanding the known to areas of the yet unknown. The awarding of the terminal or highest degree is based on the students having pushed knowledge a little or a lot, and having thus transformed the unknown into the known. The student describes this new understanding in a dissertation of several hundreds of pages, and his or her university formally accepts it and enters it into its library as a fully approved volume. If the student can find a commercial publisher, he or she is free to sign a contract and the dissertation is revised and sent to bookstores and to Amazon.com.

Countless grants and awards are given for success in the discovering or creating of that which was unknown or not yet done. This concern for the authentically new is one of the fundamental reasons for the abhorrence in universities of anything like plagiarism, which involves the theft of another person's research and imagination. I, personally, would far prefer for a thief to steal my property than for him or her to steal the few relationships and theories that I have spent a lifetime assembling and articulating for the first time. If I had never been born, these relationships and theories just might have never been seen. In an infinitesimal manner, I have participated in the apparently endless expansion of the cosmos.

Academia

This world of the university is known by the word "academia," which comes from Latin. For many years, this was the language spoken by many persons who used it to communicate with scholars in other parts of the world that had their own first languages. It should come as no surprise to anyone that a unique, formal, and relatively uniform style of writing should have evolved. "Academic writing" is very different from the writing of novels, short stories, dramas, poems, letters, political speeches, formal treaties between countries, introductions of guest speakers, comedy routines, news stories, feature articles, song lyrics, and the like. Each culture develops expectations concerning each of these different kinds of writing. This is certainly true of the kinds of things written about in academia and of the manners of writing that are appropriate.

In this small book, we are considering only one of these accepted manners of writing. The one approach we will focus on is clearly not the only one that is acceptable in other academic situations and in other classes. However, if we study several kinds of academic writing, we will probably master none. Therefore, in my class, we will study only the one presented below. If we work at it for a period of 14 weeks, we will probably come close to achieving a basic ability to use it fluently. If we master this single approach, we will be able to vary its constituents intelligently in a manner acceptable to most teachers. Besides, if you do master this single approach, virtually all undergraduate and graduate instructors will be delighted.

The Basic Approach

The basic approach we will use is almost embarrassingly simple. It contrasts (1) a presently used method of doing or thinking about something with (2) a method that is not presently used but that is advocated. And it presents categories of reasons for considering the second method preferable to the first. That's it. For convenience, we can call the first approach "old"; and the second approach, "new." Or, we can call the first, "the approach that will be replaced," and the second, "the approach that we consider better." In our considerations, we will recommend certain steps in the progression from "old" to "new."

We will also look at the "rubric" or set of measurements used by some teachers in determining if a particular term paper meets or fails to meet the requirements of their department. It is crucial that what is taught is directly related to the rubric by which we teachers evaluate the writing and general performance of our students. If a student sees insufficient relationship between the teaching and the rubric, then he or she is justified in challenging a grade. Therefore, after discussing the presentation of the "old" and the "new," in Chapter 11 we will consider in detail the relationship between the term paper and the rubric.

###

Chapter 6:
Imagination and the New

New ideas are always imaginative. Imagination is part of the bedrock of science. Although highly spoken of by Albert Einstein, the imagination is sometimes referred to as frivolous and insubstantial by contemporary scientists and theoreticians. That is indeed regrettable: one can only assume that these men and women were allowing the association between "imagination" and the arts to overwhelm their understanding of references to the "Aha!" moment when two or more previously unrelated concepts somehow became conflated and a way forward opened. Call that moment what you will, it marks a significant advance in the intellectual history of the human race.

There is a strong relation between the imagination as (1) an intellectual tool of scientific discovery and (2) a fanciful prediction of possibilities that have not yet come about. It is the responsibility of the writer-scientist to make certain that he/she is vigilant in maintaining the distinction. On the practical level of foresight, George Orwell in the novel *1984* imaginatively predicted the political oppression that afflicts the contemporary world. The first landing site on the planet Mars was recently named for the late writer Ray Bradbury, whose imagination had allowed him to write with stunning clarity about the journey to that planet long before such a trip was an actuality. In a deeper reference, we see that concentration, information and the heightened imagination work together to yield some amazing theories and predictions that physicists, for example, strive to verify, often using phrases like "Absolute Elsewhere" to refer to an obscure area in their scientific research.

Of course--for the term paper--imagination without evidence to support it is idle and virtually without value. It is definitely negative when we feel that our idea is new but that it is very special and needs no evidence. That discipline--allowing the scientist to speak about only what was the result of a hypothesis--has proven to be itself among the most significant advances man as a species has yet made. Those two premises--the hypothesis and objective evidence--are at the center of the scientific method.

The Old as New

The new idea can very well be of new relationships. For example, last weekend, I attended an exhibition of Chinese art objects from the 12th Century A.D. in New York City. In itself, this is definitely not new. However, I saw one fascinating part of the exhibit that dealt with theater and travelling troupes. In that section, I saw paintings and sculpture depicting Chinese theatre troupes that traveled from town to town. These theatre companies enacted on the stage the roles of characters that were then well known in the vast culture of China. It struck me that these troupes were amazingly similar to troupes active in Europe, particularly Italy during the same period of the early Renaissance in Europe. If this similarity has not been observed before, it would be highly suitable as a topic--not only for a freshman term paper but possibly for a doctoral dissertation--the culminating paper many students must write before receiving their terminal degree.

Such a topic fulfills the requirement of the paper we are describing: the whole thrust of the argument is guided by a hypothesis, a new theory about something that the writer has seen or suspects to be true. The five parts we have been discussing--(1) convincing the reader, (2) changing widely held opinions, (3) using objective evidence, (4) discussing the "old" idea, and (5) supporting a new hypothesis—generally constitute a typical academic paper. This is closely related to the scientific approach, which has become a central characteristic of thinking in contemporary universities.

It might be noted that some contemporary readers hold that there is no such thing as objective evidence. They maintain that all evidence results from a personal decision. For example, our deciding exactly what we will measure reflects a personal choice and invalidates the notion that the evidence is objective, that is, non-personal. Such an argument, however, is specious: i.e., it is not as good as it sounds. Without doubt, there is a point at which the personal enters any argument. This does not render that argument invalid: when Jonas Salk finally claimed to have developed a vaccine that would prevent polio, it did in fact prevent polio. There might have been something personal that entered his basic argument, but that did not invalidate his research, which was expressed in academic writing.

###

Chapter 7:
Titles, Subheads and Conclusion

It is interesting that although the title is a very important part of any piece of writing, student papers often do not have one. They just begin writing and possibly revising, then handing the paper in--with no title. The main reason a title is important has to do with expectations. When we expect something, we tend to understand it better. Therefore, the title should be a clear indication of what the paper will be about. Be careful not to have a title like "Hollywood Lifestyles" and then write mainly about movies. The word "lifestyle" means the kind of things one does when he or she is not working. In a movie, we see actors at work. Your paper should be either about actors when they are working or when they are at leisure. If you want the paper to be about both, you should alter the title to: "Hollywood: Lifestyles and Acting."

One popular style of title involves the colon[:]. The words before the colon are often taken from the thesis. For example, "Rock Lyrics: The Literature our Students Listen To" (Moi, 1998). The colon can be roughly interpreted as an equals sign [=] in mathematics, or as the linking verbs "is, are" in language. Convention does not permit us to use a complete sentence as the title: the colon helps to circumvent that prohibition. If we attempt to ignore the prohibition, we will be marked as uninformed. Neither should the titles of academic papers be colorful and fanciful. "Pronouns and Pro-Puppies" is an example of a smart-sounding title that has one fatal error--it does not indicate what the paper is about.

Subheads

The title will be the main "head" of your paper. "Subheads" are the names of smaller sections of that paper. For example, if "Hollywood Lifestyles" is the title; then the subheads might be "Dating," "Hobbies," "Reading" and "Nightlife." Each subhead is like a small title for one part of your paper. In an academic research paper such as you will write, you will normally use subheads derived from the categories we discussed earlier. You will use 12-point boldface font for the major subheads, and 12-point regular font for smaller subheads. The rule of thumb is that when you have one major subhead, you will have two or more major subheads. When you have one minor subhead in regular font, you will have at least two minor subheads. I am giving you a precise set of specifications. If you vary one, the whole will be affected. Therefore, you do not have the freedom to do as you like. Or rather, you can do as you like: just be prepared for a low grade. Forewarned is forearmed.

In Regard to Concluding

The main purpose of the conclusion is to tell the reader that the paper is ending. It is wise to do this because of the deep human affinity for things that have a beginning, a middle and an end. A paper that is academic and not literary still works in an ambience that is found in virtually all human structures that deal with time. So, if your writing is in the form of a short story or an acceptance speech for a Nobel Prize, you need a beginning, a middle and an end.

Often, mentioning a detail from the very beginning of the paper will serve to do that. For example, your paper dealt with the increase in the awareness of the apparent effectiveness of herbs and food supplements. You might have started the paper with Ponce de Leon's search for a magical "Fountain of Youth." Your old idea was that many contemporary physicians were taught in medical school to rely solely on manufactured drugs that have been approved by the U.S. Government. Your new idea concerns reports by reputable sources that food supplements made from real vegetable and fruits seem to be surprisingly effective. In the conclusion, one sentence of reference to the "Fountain of Youth" serves to demonstrate that you are aware of the sophistication that is associated with this method of ending the paper.

****

Figure 3. Repeating Detail in Conclusion: This is an illustration of the technique of mentioning some detail in the very first sentence of the paper, and then repeating that detail (here, Ponce de Leon) in the conclusion to indicate that the paper is at an end.

Herbs and Supplements:
An Old Lesson being Relearned
by
Harold P. Essingbo

Introduction

Ponce de Leon had great faith in his dream of a magical fountain that would prolong life. In a sense, many contemporary physicians seem to have a similar greater faith in medicines that are commercially produced than in the herbs and food supplements that have recently been reported to be remarkably effective.

xxxxxxxxxxxxx
xxxxxxxxxxxxx
xxxxxxxxxxxxx

Conclusion

When Ponce de Leon was searching all over Florida for the magical spring that would make humans live longer, he would have been surprised to find that the secret was in the plants all around him. *[Your conclusion might also contain a brief restatement of the thesis and possibly the categories which you named.]*

****

Beginning with the Conclusion

When you write your conclusion, you will have thought and talked about your topic many times. As a result, you might well understand that topic better than when you wrote the introduction. If your conclusion is stronger and better articulated than your introduction, you should consider using it in the introduction and writing another conclusion. In my professional editing, I have encountered this phenomenon from time to time in articles that dealt with the imagination. Every time I did so, the author agreed that the conclusion worked better as the introduction.

No Saving the Best for Last

It is also very important that you do not save the best part of your research for presentation in the last part of your paper. In academic writing, that is disaster. We should put the best, most persuasive sentences in the introduction, very near the beginning of the paper. This principle might be the opposite of what is considered good style in different countries. When in Rome, do as the Romans do.

Chapter 8:
Naming the Categories

The first point I would like to make in this chapter is that all categories come from the thesis statement. Ideally, all of the main categories in a paper are to be found in that statement. For example, my theoretical term paper will have the following hypothesis: "When mothers are sent to prison, the punishment they endure is far more widespread than when single men are incarcerated for an equal length of time." The following categories present themselves: (1) Conditions in prison for women, (2) Absence of mothers from families, (3) Embarrassment of families, and (4) Loss of self-esteem by mothers themselves, and (5) Single male prisoners. The first category that we called "Conditions" might well be broken down into the following features (See Chapter 14): A. Attitudes of inmates; B. Attitudes of guards; C. Physical difficulties of confinement, and D. Lonliness. Each category can be broken down into features. Then, each feature can become a category and be broken down into features.

Approached in this fashion, the organization of the entire term paper is indicated. This Category/Feature breakdown can be projected through the imagination: all aspects of it, however, must be substantiated through research. If there is not sufficient evidence for any category or feature, that category or feature must be deleted. In similar fashion, if evidence for an unnamed category or feature presents itself, then that category or feature must be added. Our exploration of the hypothesis concerning mothers who are in prison must be amenable to evidence. The constant change in balance between the title, the hypothesis and the evidence is the primary rule that must be rigorously observed if the inherent and ongoing strength of the argument is to be realized.

The two preceding paragraphs are of great interest to the writer. They might well be framed and placed on the wall above your computer or writing area. At least for the duration of this course.

Naming as a Process

Many individual items of information often make little or no sense if they are presented en masse, with no order or organization present. I am talking about items such as the following: one inch wide, reddish-blue, two feet high, clear, large, angry, young, blue, plastic, term papers, academic, sophisticated, casual, chatty, fig-shaped and so on. If, however, I suggest categories such as size, shape, color, psychological characteristics, and manner, I can place these items into groups. Categorizing is not rocket science—at least at first. However, rocket scientists might well disagree on whether a certain process should be placed in this or that category based on properties displayed. In that case--as in a great many others--categorization is very often of truly great importance. Later in this book, we will consider the crucial observation of African-American Dexter Jeffries that "race" is not fact but an "artificial category" that has no lexical or "word-like" features.

A great deal of academic writing is concerned with precisely this matter: Does this or that item belong in this or that category? One primary reason for this importance is that much of our thinking involves categorization. That is why the naming of categories is so very important. For us, categories play an immensely important role in organizing the different pieces of evidence we find in different sources. If we have four tentative categories, we can list in each category the relevant information that we find in different books, magazines, interviews, movies, websites, blogs, journals and surveys.

Sometimes it is wise to divide a large composition book into sections in which we list evidence supporting a particular point. For example, if our term paper discusses the main reasons for the banning of football from school sports, we can name one section, "Injuries"; another, "Culture of Violence: another, "Expense" and the last, "Effect on Academics." In each section, we will enter the information that we can use to support the reason we are discussing in that section. More precisely, if section three supports reasons related to "Expense," we will not--in that section--be concerned with "Violence" or with "Injuries." We will, in that third section, be interested only in issues related to money.

A category is like a division: if we divide something, we always have at least two parts. If we divide a topic, we always have at least two categories. The word "category" refers to the content that is divided, Categories are made by persons and do not exist apart from people. Categories always have their origin in a topic as a common feature. For example, most dogs, cats, rabbits, chickens, ducks and geese can be grouped into a single topic: they all have something covering most or all of their skin. Dogs, cats and rabbits have a common feature--hair covering most of their bodies. On the other hand, chickens, ducks and geese are covered with feathers. If we classify these creatures according to *hair* and to *feathers*, we will have two categories.

The main goal of this chapter is to illustrate the great wisdom involved in initially reducing these categories to countable names because of our wish to present a compelling argument that can be comprehended. Our expansion of the names into fully developed categories will allow the reader to at least perceive our possible coherence. By far, the most important reason for assembling things and dividing them into categories is that they are all relevant to what we are claiming is something new. If we are writing a term paper and wish to discuss our new thesis, it is essential to base the similarities on the new idea.

The Principle of Naming

To discuss the very important principle of "naming categories," we will pretend that we are working for a manufacturer of tools. There is a new idea afloat. Some Young Turks in our company want us to give all of our energy to the conversion to power tools operated by gasoline and electricity. They say the hand tools--on which our company was established 200 years ago-- are old fashioned and should be discontinued. We comprise another faction in the company who thinks that they are wrong. Our group has called a major meeting with the President of our company and the Board of Directors to discuss the matter.

We have sought the advice of an Older Gentleman who is not too bad at organizing such presentation. He is on our side. After several meetings, we have decided that there are six categories in which our evidence can be summarized. Those categories are the following:

1. **Hand tools are not as expensive as power tools,**
2. **Hand tools usually last longer,**
3. **Hand tools are sometimes easier to control than power tools,**
4. **The quality of work done with hand tools is often higher,**
5. **A personal relationship often develops between hand tools and the craftsman.**
6. **The integrity of our company goes back to a time when there was no such thing as a "power tool." It would be a mistake to sever the tie between high quality and handmade tools.**

All of the categories are closely related to the question, "Why should our company continue to produce hand tools?" We could easily write two pages on each of the six categories. However, condensing these 12 pages into less than half of one page make for a more dynamic presentation to the Board of Directors and the President of the company. Everyone appreciates having a short list instead of a long list, at least at the beginning. In the opinion of the Older Gentleman, this presentation might also be improved by <u>reversing</u> the order in which the six categories are presented: i.e., Item Number 6 would become Item Number 1, and so on.

The Crucial Names

The older gentleman takes us aside, checks to make certain that no one else is listening, and then takes a deep breath and whispers as though he were telling us a deep, dark secret. He says that there is something else that just might increase the dynamic nature of our presentation. All of us asked, "What? What?" He looks at each of us slowly and carefully and then reveals his wisdom. "You can," he says, "increase interest even further by "naming" each of the categories, which could then be brought into a single sentence. He then smiles a little and asks, "Do you understand?" No, we say. "What are you talking about? Have you gone crazy?" The Older Gentleman then stands up and tells us to be seated. He clears his throat and says slowly and distinctly:

"There are six major reasons why our company should not only continue but develop and enhance our attention to hand tools: (1) integrity, (2) personal relationships, (3) high quality of work, (4) ease of control, (5) durability, and (6) expense."

"This is 'naming'," he said. It is one of the most valuable tools or organizing that I have ever seen. Once you have decided on the most important part of each piece of evidence, you must name it. After you have named it, you can expand each name." He then left the room and we decided that he was right.

Our old idea was that our company should discontinue the production of tools designed to work by hand and without gasoline or electricity. Our new idea is that the production of such tools should not only be continued but enhanced. As background, we could briefly discuss the founding of the company and the gradual increase in the number of power tools we have produced. Our presentation would be factual and not tainted by negative terminology. In academic writing, a factor of personal meaning is not allowed: it spoils the most elegant of arguments and presentations. In other situations, however, it can be relevant and effective. Therefore, the first category would be "integrity" followed by "personal relationships" and so on.

Our conclusion would be short but effective. What we would have done is use the academic structure we are discussing in this book for commercial application.

Design and Illustration

We might re-structure our presentation into a long and tedious sequence of words and sentences. Yet a large number of words with no design elements or illustrations will be a little like gulping and beginning our swim across the wide Mississippi River. Having a place to stop and something to look at will make our job of convincing the Board and the President much easier. In the pages that follow, I will attempt to introduce such elements as best I can. However, I am not a Graphic Designer--a person who draws patterns on paper, nor am I an artist.

If I am putting together a paper for my company which produces tools, I will at least attempt to find a person who knows about graphic design and another who knows about illustration. Together, we will be able to turn out an attractive, dynamic product that will advance our cause. Term papers do not have amateurish fonts and random photographs cut from comic books: such elements will have a negative effect. Be careful with imaginative design and illustrations: always check with your instructor or supervisor before attempting to use them.

Chapter 9:
The Necessary Hypothesis

The academic paper does not concern itself with expressing the opinions and feelings of the author about a given topic. Neither is it concerned with whether the writer is heavy or thin, cheats at card games, gossips, drinks too much alcohol, or does not practice personal hygiene. The only important issues are whether the writer's hypothesis is well articulated and is supported by objective evidence gained through such things as experiments, interviews, surveys, books, newspapers, magazines, and internet sources that are carefully chosen and arranged.

The academic paper does not simply assemble and present related information on a particular topic such as the following: "Food eaten at children's birthday parties in different parts of the world." Although this topic might well be fascinating, it does not really qualify as academic writing. There is a critical reason for this. In the kind of term paper we are describing, we are concerned with argumentation based on the careful presentation of objective, <u>verifiable evidence guided by a hypothesis, or new theory.</u> If we discuss food and nothing more, then there is little or no hypothesis involved. On the other hand, new theories are part of the very heart of the scientific approach to the natural world. Nowhere is this approach more honored and respected than in the university.

Academic Discourse

Academic writing is part of academic discourse. This is a formal, precise, and highly patterned style of language use. Unfortunately, it is rarely taught--or even studied--overtly as a desirable style. Yet virtually everyone who goes through graduate school comes to recognize it as very effective and at least tries to use it in the execution of academic writing. In addition, it is an important signal to other educators and researchers that the writer is familiar with academic discourse and can express his or her ideas accordingly. In other words, the ability to use academic discourse serves as a valuable marker of an expert. If we want to change the way people think about something, it is necessary that we first convince them (1) that we know what we are talking about, and (2) that we are capable of expressing ourselves in a manner that they recognize as their own.

Religion and Romance

In academia, we approach the world as something that can be successfully studied and learned about according to specific objective evidence. There are other kinds of thinking that are completely different--for example, religion and romance. In a romantic novel or poem, the author is concerned with--among other things--telling a story of people in love with other people or with an ideal, not with presenting evidence that his or her new theory is accurate and valid. Religion is often concerned with a person's relationship with a deity. The evidence presented in romantic or religious writing is *subjective* in nature. For example, I might have been profoundly shaken by my vision of an angel. I may want to sing and shout about this experience, yet the experience produces nothing that can be measured by a person who has not had my vision of an angel. In that case, I cannot use in my academic paper any part of the experience, which is subjective.

If the author and I have similar emotional feelings about older parents, we will not have to do anything to convince other that we are right. We will simply refer to our convictions: that is enough. Frankly, we do not care if anyone believes us or not. However, little if any of the evidence we discuss falls under the classification *"objective and/or verifiable"* through measureable experiments and impersonal observations that can be repeated by other persons. There is nothing wrong with writing that follows other pipers, but we must be careful to avoid allowing it to interfere with our formal approach to academic writing and the strict standards it demands.

Science is not concerned with the personal qualities of the writer. It is very much concerned with clear thinking, the logical presentation of solid evidence, and--most of all--with the exact articulation of the thesis statement concerning a basic hypothesis. Each theory, experiment and observation is carried out as though the final truth is near--the truth that will end much doubt about the matter at hand. Scientists often approach each element in their solution to a particular problem as though it were attainable. Yet they know that their findings might well be thrown out when another better theory is developed. In this seemingly contradictory manner, science has proven to be the best approach possible at the time. In Chapter 15: Developing a Thesis, I discuss in detail the kind of idea that constitutes a thesis and how it is arrived at. This is central to a valid argumentative term paper.

Evidence for a Change in Thinking

At the risk of over-simplification, we might suggest that the writer of an essay looks inward for the source of his thoughts and comments. Academic writers, on the other hand, get their material from carefully made observations and experiments in the natural world. The ultimate goal of academic writing is the presentation of compelling evidence in an argument that might result in a change in the way that scientists and others think about something. The key term here is "argument": When Salk developed a vaccination against polio, he was trying to construct an accurate argument that he was right and that would prevent the disease from crippling or killing human beings. His evidence was based on his knowledge and research in biology. When his vaccine did in fact prevent the disease, that was the objective verification that his theory was true. The term paper is a first step in this direction.

When an instructor suggests or approves a term paper topic, he or she does not expect that that student will go the library and discover an article that is based on an articulation of that hypothesis--that in fact changes the topic from a "hypothesis" into a "thesis." It is sheer lunacy and plagiarism for the student to think that he or she can pretend the found paper has not been written but can be used as a source for the new student's term paper. If that article has already been written, then the student must go to the instructor and get another topic. The student will then attempt to develop the new hypothesis from the ground up.

This includes but is not limited to studying the internet, finding articles in magazines, finding related research in books, interviewing experts in the field, conducting experiments in laboratory, visiting classes to administer questionnaires, getting permission to speak with hospital patients or prison inmates. Up to a point, the different kinds of evidence you present will make your paper stronger and stronger. Among the basic principles of this course are (1) that you are willing to do the work that your inquiring mind comes up with, and (2) that you do not "create" evidence that sounds convincing. The latter is academically unethical and will be dealt with harshly.

New Idea vs. Old Idea

In general, if academic writers have nothing new to say, they do not write. If they wish to write about something that has not been written about previously, then they still have to give evidence that they are right. For example, if I find the unpublished manuscript of a novelist, I must present some point of view of interpretation, and I must provide evidence that I am right. I can write a narrative of what I was doing when I happened to find the old papers. Although my narrative might be interesting, it has little or no value as academic argument; that is, it does not attempt to explore and support a new hypothesis that needs to be stated and defended. Instead, it simply tells a story. If, however, I maintain that the manuscript sheds a new light on the other expressions of the well-known author, then I am again back on solid academic ground. I will, perhaps, quote part of the new novel and examine it with reference to other things that have been said about the novelist. For me, the new novel constitutes part of the natural world, and I will develop and articulate a pointed hypothesis concerning my new idea. After I have presented a compelling argument, I will refer to my hypothesis as a full "thesis."

###

Chapter 10:
Plagiarism, Theft and Term Papers

When some students approach the term paper, they begin about three days before the paper is due, and cut-and-paste from the books, magazines and other sources, some of which they put quotation marks around, followed by parentheses containing the author's last name and a page number. Then they use other parts of the various sources <u>without</u> quotation marks pretending that it was written by them. That is, precisely, one main part of the essence of plagiarism. Then they get to the last page, the bibliography--which is sometimes called "Works Cited"-- and copy the authors' names and put next to them irrelevant and made-up information as to sources. That is another aspect of plagiarism.

Sometimes, the instructor reacts primarily to the appearance of the format. At other times, he or she assumes that the student has done the work that is implied. At yet other times, the instructor can be heard to say, "This is only a freshman class and our expectations can easily be too high. After all, some professors themselves practice plagiarism." Sometimes, those professors get away with it. At other times, they are caught and are terribly embarrassed.

An instance of plagiarism occurred at New Jersey City University in 2011. The offending party was an associate professor and president of the local chapter of the American Federation of Teachers (AFT). The person who discovered the offense was another professor from NJCU. The apology was printed in the newsletter *AFTerthoughts* on page 1 and continued on page 6 in the Spring/Summer issue of 2012.

> *Earlier this semester, [Professor] Laura Wadenpfuhl made what I know was a very difficult phone call. One of our colleagues brought to her attention the fact that I had plagiarized in my article for the fall/winter issue of* AFTerthoughts. *I included some sentences and phrases that I took from the* Occupy Wall Street *website without either footnoting them or giving the source.*
>
> *At the time I was preparing the article, I was dealing serious health issues. I dropped the ball. I neglected to give credit where credit was due. I had no intention to deceive. My mistakes were* de minimis, *however. I apologize to the editors of AFTerthoughts, the Union, and to our academic community.* (signed) *In solidarity; Ivan S. Steinberg, President; AFT Local 1839.*

It is to Prof. Steinberg's credit that he did not attempt to deny his action. As a member of the NJCU academic community, I, for one and for what it is worth, sincerely appreciate and accept the apology. Undoubtedly, the reason he felt that an apology was in order was that plagiarism is, without question, one of the worst offenses that can be committed by anyone in the academic community.

Honesty and integrity are essential to the basic principles of scientific research, which is generally held to be the cornerstone of contemporary higher education. It is absolutely essential that objective findings not be altered to fit the researcher's theories about the part of reality that he or she is studying. To do so is not "bad" science, it is not science: it is shameful, unprincipled behavior. Most plagiarism involves the conscious stealing of another person's thoughts. words and often overwhelming efforts at research itself.. The fact that the person who shamed himself by committing plagiarism was a member of the NJCU faculty does by no means diminish the culpability involved, nor does it make it "okay" for students to do what this teacher did. In any course that I teach, I will give a failing grade to any student who is guilty of substantial and verifiable plagiarism. Forewarned is forearmed.

An act that is closely related to plagiarism is the conscious insertion of false information in an official statement: this is referred to as "resume padding," that is, supposedly improving one's academic background at the expense of honesty and integrity. An example of this is claiming to have been awarded an academic degree when no such degree was awarded. Sometimes, thirty years after the plagiaristic offense, when someone is running for a political office, a diligent member of the opposition finds the offence which had been almost forgotten about by the offender. That diligent member copies the original term paper and the cited sources, and brings this evidence of malfeasance to the attention of a reporter who checks it and write a story with a great big headline: "Candidate Admits Plagiarism." The candidate's honesty and basic character is questioned. That candidate can either deny it or apologize for it and probably lose a great many votes as a result. In short, plagiarism is a serious offense against the ethics of the university: don't do it.

Chapter 11:
Rubrics and Evaluation

"Rubric" is a Latin word meaning "a concise statement of procedure." In recent years, it has been applied to "a concise or very short statement concerning evaluation." Often, it involves particular, named categories that must be checked as "PRESENT" or "ABSENT." According to a simple procedure, this will result in a number that has enormous relevance for the student whose writing is being evaluated: If the number is above a certain point, the student will pass the course. If the number is below that point, the student will be advised to take the course again. Through the use of rubrics, a group of instructors can usually reach a conclusion that is uniform, appropriate and just. I kept this rubric in the forefront of my mind as I was writing this book. Immediately below, I present an exact copy of the rubric that will be used to evaluate your paper as acceptable or unacceptable (Mabry, 2012). If I were you, I would study it very carefully.

New Jersey City University ESL Program

Writing Skills Assessment Form: Research Papers

Course: _____   Semester: _____

Content	Poor	Acceptable	Excellent
	No clear thesis statement. Topic is poorly developed, with supporting details that are absent or vague. Trite ideas and/or unclear wording reflect lack of understanding of topic and audience.	There is a thesis statement but it is difficult to locate or not clearly stated. Topic is evident with some supporting details; generally meets requirements of assignment.	There is a clearly distinguishable thesis statement. Topic is well developed, effectively supported and appropriate for the assignment.
	1 2 3 4 5		
Organization:	**Poor**	**Acceptable**	**Excellent**
	Writing is rambling and unfocused, with main theme and supporting details presented in a disorganized, unrelated way.	Writing demonstrates some grasp of organization, with a discernible theme and supporting details	Writing is clearly organized around a central theme. Each paragraph is clear and relates to the others in a well-planned framework.
	1 2 3 4 5		

39

Language	**Poor**	**Acceptable**	**Excellent**
	Writing lacks sentence variety. Significant deficiencies in wording, spelling, grammar, punctuation, or presentation.	Some sentence variety; adequate usage of wording, grammar, and punctuation.	Wide variety of sentence structures. Excellent word usage, spelling, grammar and punctuation. Effective integration of information.

1	2	3	4	5

(con't on next

Documentation	**Poor**	**Acceptable**	**Excellent**
	Paper has sources cited in text and/or sources cited on Works Cited page that do not conform to MLA or APA; the Works Cited page may be missing altogether; the sources used do not support the previous point; the sources are either over- or under-cited; the paper is plagiarized.	Paper has sources cited in text and/or sources cited on Works Cited page that show some familiarity with MLA or APA but the errors are noticeable; the sources used somewhat support the previous point; sources may be over- or under-cited; the paper is plagiarized in places.	Paper demonstrates ability to incorporate sources within the text, and an ability to document sources on a Works Cites page using MLA or APA style; the sources used directly support the previous point; the sources are not over- or under-cited. The paper is not plagiarized.

1	2	3	4	5

Overall Comments: _____**Points:** ____/20**

NOTE: Students must achieve at least a 3 in each area to demonstrate proficiency.

Revised 04/03/12

The four categories of evaluation are indicated on the left of the printed rubric. They are the following: (1) Content, (2) Organization, (3) Language, and (4) Documentation. It is possible for an evaluator to check one of five performance ratings for each category. "Students must achieve at least a 3 in each area [or category] to demonstrate proficiency." Theoretically, this means that if you score a 5 in three areas and a 2 in the fourth, you will be asked to take the course again. This virtually never happens: students who score 5 in one area will almost always score 3 or above in the others. You should, however, observe how seriously your teachers take both term papers and this rubric.

Content

In this book, we will look fairly closely at each of the four categories in the rubric. First, we will comment on "Content" and later devote a chapter to each of the following: Organization, Language and Documentation. "Content" refers to your hypothesis and to the evidence you cite to make it turn into a proper thesis. Under the label "Poor" for this area, there is written: ***"No clear thesis statement. Topic is poorly developed, with supporting details that are abstract or vague. Trite ideas and/or unclear wording reflect lack of understanding of topic and audience."*** Your instructor will explain any of these faults that you do not understand. We will point out that "topic" here means all that is contained in the thesis sentence. In the paper we are describing, the categories of evidence should support the thesis sentence.

Under the label "Acceptable," there is written: ***"There is a thesis statement but it is difficult to locate or not clearly stated. Topic is evident with some supporting details; generally meets requirements of assignments."*** "Excellent" is the third and final demonstration of proficiency: ***"There is a clearly distinguishable thesis statement. Topic is well developed, effectively supported and appropriate for the assignment."*** Now, we will concentrate on the critical area of thesis statement, which is given as a prime criterion in each of the above. It is virtually impossible to over-emphasize the importance of the thesis. In Chapter 12, we will stress different components of the thesis statement and offer an example. In Chapter 15, we will discuss the process of arriving at an acceptable thesis statement using a six-item checklist.

###

Chapter 12:
The Thesis Statement

Possibly the most important part of academic writing is the quality of the "thesis statement." The thesis is the new idea that we are saying should replace the old idea. It is the central linchpin that connects the new with the old, and in so doing insures that the writer is on solid academic ground. This connection must be crystal clear, and it must be succinctly articulated in the "thesis statement." This is central to our presentation in this book as it is to the rubric we use to evaluate student writing. If we do not identify what is old and what is new, then our term paper will possibly be mediocre at best. It should be remembered that the distinction between the old idea and the new idea is one that I have set up and that I am requiring that you follow. Another teacher might say that it is not necessary to make this distinction. I am convinced, however, that the old/new distinction is one excellent notion for an undergraduate to develop.

For example, at one time boxing was considered a sport that was appropriate in schools. Now boxing is considered inappropriate, mainly because it is too dangerous, at least in elementary and high school. At the time boxing was considered appropriate, an interesting paper could have been written about the reasons it should be banned from the schools. Many parents, students, and coaches would have said that we were wrong. To support our position, we would have to name several major reasons for claiming that boxing should be prohibited. In this paper, we will refer to such reasons as "categories of evidence."

To discuss only the danger of physical injury would constitute a meaningful paper. After all, the basis for winning in boxing is the amount of physical damage one person does to his opponent. More precisely put, the important thing is the number of times he hits the opponent's face or body and the number of times he avoids being hit by footwork or guarding by the hands and arms. If we were actually writing a paper on boxing, we would put here the name and page number of our source(s). In our bibliography, we would expand this to include the title, the publisher, the place of publication and similar items of information.

However, the idea that boxing has the blessings of tradition is a strong argument for not banning the activity. And it is good to have a strong opposition: it means that we will have to find several other categories of evidence that support our criticism of boxing. If we read more widely, we might come up with three other categories which we can summarize in the following manner: (1) Physical Injury, (2) Learned Aggression, and (3) Confused Identity. Let us consider these briefly. Physical injury seems near the heart of boxing. The winner hits his opponent more often and in more places than does his opponent. Outside the boxing ring, that kind of behavior can easily be a reason for imprisonment.

Direct and Indirect Evidence

A very troubling effect of boxing is the learning of aggression which is said to intrude on normal relationships. We must look for information on this point that can help support our contention. This information need not mention boxing itself: the negative relationships between aggression and social behavior would be sufficient. This brings up an important point: your evidence need not mention boxing. It must, however, bear witness to a truth that will apply to boxing or whatever argument you are making. This way of accumulating direct and indirect evidence will serve to strengthen considerably the precise argument you are building. We must be diligent about keeping the reader informed of the relation between our evidence and our basic argument. Some cultures might not require this direct illustration: the academic culture does.

Identity refers to an intimate part of the sense of who we are. To some degree, this sense seems to be inborn. However, our particular society can have a powerful influence on what we consider acceptable or unacceptable behavior. Boxing can lead some people to consider the most violent person to be the most successful. We set up these individuals and want to act like them-- the "heroes" we can identify with in the world of boxing. Yet this identity is not in accord with "inborn identity" and the identity we formed in our families when we were growing up. Boxing would seem to promote a confusion of the two identities in the individual.

Imagination and Analysis

Imagination is very important to the process of analysis. However, unless we find evidence to support our imaginative ideas, they are worse than useless in our academic writing. In personal essays, on the other hand, the imagination is very valuable. The two kinds of writing- -academic research and personal expression--are very different and should not be confused. In my armchair, I can come up with even more categories. But it is vitally necessary that in academic writing, I support each category with substantial evidence that I can get from reading books, magazines, newspapers, and journals. I can also interview older persons who were boxers or coaches. I can present any information that I get from watching television or listening to the radio. I can use relevant movies like *Rocky*. I can count the number of comic books--now called "graphic novels"--that tacitly endorse boxing. In fact, I can use almost any source of information about the sport. This information is not necessarily in support of my position, but will be used by me in the citation and construction of my larger argument--that boxing should be banned.

Example of Thesis Statement

An acceptable thesis statement could be the following:

Boxing should be banned from elementary and high school sports, primarily because of the physical, mental, and moral damage it can cause.

You will notice that I have summarized the evidence present in the four categories. This is wise and good.

Nota Bene

In Latin, "nota bene" means "note well." You should note well that if you find a source that makes exactly the case against boxing that you support, then you must change or modify your topic. Why? Because your argument has already been made: it is no longer new. To use all of the information you find in that article and say that you have found and assembled that information is plagiarism. If you do this and get an "A" on your paper, you will know that your grade should be "F" and that you have acted without honor and stolen the research of another person. If that makes you no difference, then you should withdraw from the university at once because you are dishonest and a cheat, and do not belong in an institution that values honesty and integrity.

If you did assemble the information and make the argument yourself, you should be proud to indicate where the future reader of your term paper can go if he or she wants more information. Possibly, that person will want to make certain that you did not create the evidence out of only your imagination. The university is well aware of the importance of your saying where you found the evidence and calls this process "documentation." We will look more closely at this process later in this book.

If you gather your information and some of it does not support your hypothesis, you should mention that in the "Background" (Chapter 21). Everyone in academia is aware that some of your research findings will likely not support your hypothesis. Do not attempt to hide these findings or--heaven forbid--change them to fit your hypothesis. You are to enter them as part of the description of the present attitude toward your topic. If, however, the preponderance of your research supports the present attitude and not your thesis, then you will have to change your hypothesis or alter it so that it still deals with something new. Or, you have to change topics. You should see your instructor about this.

###

Chapter 13:
Categories and Critical Thinking

Categories represent one of the fundamental characteristic of Western thinking-analysis. When we analyze something, we take it apart to see how it works. The opposite of analysis is "synthesis," putting two or more things together to make a new entity. Both analysis and synthesis are necessary in writing academic term papers: we analyze that which currently exists in order to determine the categories involved. If we are not satisfied with the answer, we add to or rearrange the categories in order to achieve a new way of thinking. Much of education is concerned with learning the current explanations which are regarded as "facts" and adding to or rearranging them to arrive at new explanations. Many if not most of these items of information are in a state of constant flux. The purpose of the academy is to maintain order in that flux and to try to insure that all changes have substantial reasons. This is the scientific method.

The ability to analyze, recognize, and create categories has great value today and is often referred to as "Critical Thinking." The danger with critical thinking is the assumption often made that it can be used in a straightforward and fairy simple search for truth--that is, for facts that do not change. As we have seen, however, that kind of truth does not exist: it seems to be a false model of the world. So that, from one point of view, "Critical Thinking" can often be seen as a "buzz-word," that is, a term that comes into widespread use in a short period of time, and that the user of the term is or wants to be accepted as a member of a group that is socially approved.

Serious analysis usually requires a lot of careful thinking. Let us consider the idea that "All races are equal." This seems like a straightforward and just statement. If we want to analyze the statement, we might observe that the word "race" normally refers to such things as average weight and height; color of skin, hair and eyes; shape of skull; average width of nose and lips; and several other things that can be tested for. If I say that "All races are equal," I am basing my statement on the idea that there is indeed such a thing as race. Also, if I say that two things are equal, I am affirming that they are not the same. If they were the same, then they could not be said to be equal.

	Feature 1: __FOUR FEET__
	Feature 2: __NOCTURNALLY ACTIVE__
	Feature 3: __FUR__
Name of Category: __CAT__	**Feature 4:** __EYES IN FRONT__
	Feature 5: __RETRACTABLE NAILS__
	Feature 6-n: __LONG WHISKERS (etc.)__

To better understand what we are now going to say about Dexter Jeffries, I think it wise to call your attention to "lexical structure," which we will discuss in more detail in the following chapter. The word "lexical" means simply "relating to words." The chart I present immediately above is concerned with the meaning of a word. "Cat" means something that has the features of "four feet, fur" etc.

What Jeffries, an African-American, says is that the word "race" has no meaning. It took him a long time to see that, but now he does. In other words, he had used "race" as though it were a legitimate concept. After talking with a therapist for a long time, he had an "epiphany"-- or sudden realization--that "race" has no features. There is no meaning involved. The word, he said, did not represent a legitimate concept as does the word "cat."

> From that day, I kept on the main track with only some minor digressions. She helped me to understand who I was, from a humane point of view. <u>And when it comes down to it, race is not human; it's an artificial categorization employed to justify what is inherently human: weakness, fear, diffidence and timidity.</u> [Underlines are by Coreil.] By focusing on the human side--my family, my relationships with my father, mother, brother and sister--I was able to make some substantial progress in consolidating a genuine identity. (Raimes, 224)

What Jeffries did was to think critically about a concept, race, and find that at least in some uses, it did not mean what people usually assume that it means. He had to struggle with the meaning of a word that he had assumed was a correct part of the analysis of the world. Ultimately, he rejected the category called "race" and, by extension, that part of the process of critical thinking that is based on race. He implies but does not ask this seemingly relevant question: What is the relation between culture and race? Does pigmentation overwhelm the apparent difference between a native-born citizen of Ethiopia and a native-born black citizen of New York?

A more pointed issue concerns the following question: Within the same "race," can minimal differences in culture acquire the magnitude normally associated with the word, race? For an answer, one need look no further than the continent of Africa and the apparently mutual hatred of the Hutus for the Tutsies, whose main difference was not even apparently a matter of language or religion. The absence of racial differences did not prevent the murder of up to one million people in a pogrom based on essentially imagined differences. Personally, I would take Jeffries' position that "race is not human; it's an artificial categorization...."

Following the rules of syntax or grammar, one can put together concepts like "racial superiority," "intellectual inferiority," "ethnic cleansing," "inferiority complex" and "critical thinking." Before we accept any of these ideas as valid, we should examine them and their constituent features carefully. That is precisely what term papers are designed to do--examine ideas closely and carefully, and change them on the basis of external evidence.

Black Bear Speaks

Another example of this phenomenon is reported by Kathleen Gaffney (2003) who reports an instance where she had been discussing the arts to an assembly of Native Americans. "I had been speaking for only ten minutes when from the back of the audience a man rose. He was Black Bear, the leader of the Black Feet, and he spoke very loudly and slowly with respect.

'Excuse me, I mean no disrespect, but we of the Black Feet have difficulty every time you say the word "art." For in our language, there is no such word. For us, what you call art is everything we are and everything we do. You Anglo's--and I mean no disrespect--have taken art out of everything and put it over there.' He pointed far away. 'But for me what you call art is my clothing, my healing, my cooking, my spirit: it is as close to me as my skin.'

(Coreil, 154)

The valuable lessons Jeffries and Black Bear teach us is that we should examine carefully every part of an argument, and that we should not stop examining it just because of a buzz-word that happens to be popular at a given time. This is not to say that critical thinking is of little value: quite the opposite. It is to say that it is demeaning for anyone to think that critical thinking can be approached and taught simplistically.

###

Chapter 14:
Categories and Lexical Structure

From time to time, one encounters the idea that writing is an essential part of thinking. Stated generally, there seems to be a valid belief that the conscious manipulation of words, meaning, phrases, sentences and paragraphs can result in a profound increase the domain of thinking. For now, that conscious manipulation of thought through language will serve as a brief definition of writing.

To my knowledge, a closer, more detailed and possibly more rewarding link between writing and thinking is yet to be explored. Therefore, I would like to speculate about one specific connection between the two processes. It is my hypothesis that at least one of the structures found in the lexicon is quite similar to the structure we have described as an effective way of analyzing and supporting a thesis statement. That is to say, it would be quite interesting if the lexicon (vocabulary) were to operate in terms of categories, each of which in turn operates in terms of sub-categories ad infinitum. In that case, the mind itself would seem to support our thesis with evidence given in general terms of categories.

In Figure 4 below, I present "Lexical Structure." In Figure 5, I fill in the blanks with lexical items or words. In Figure 6, I make the transition to academic writing.

****

Feature 1: _____

Feature 2: _____

Feature 3: _____

Name of Category: _____

Feature 4: _____

Feature 5: _____

Feature 6-n: _____

Figure 4: Representation of Lexical Structure. There is no limit to the number of features that can constitute a particular category, which here would be a particular lexical item or word. (The enumeration "6-n" means that there is no terminal point or end to the number of items that are possible.)

****

****

Feature 1: **FOUR FEET**

Feature 2: **NOCTURNALLY ACTIVE**

Feature 3: **FUR**

Name of Category: **CAT**

Feature 4: **EYES IN FRONT**

Feature 5: **RETRACTABLE NAILS**

Feature 6-n: **LONG WHISKERS (etc.)**

Figure 5: Features of Lexical Structure. If any of these features are absent, or if there are present any not found in most cats, the creature will probably be called "cat-like" and not "cat." The important point for writers is to realize that this index of characteristics is generally unconscious unless one or more of them is absent or unexpectedly present, in which case the list will become fore-fronted in the mind and conscious adjustments made. This is quite similar to what happens when we present convincing evidence that requires the construction of a new concept. (See Figure 3.) Jeffries (See above) denied reality to the word "race." In the metaphor "romance is fishing," "romance" is spoken of in the features of "fishing.

****

Evidence 1: **Danger of Physical Injury**

Evidence 2: **Over-Emphasis on Physical Strength**

Evidence 3: **Endorsement of Violence**

New Idea: **Football Should be Banned**

Evidence 4: **Little Relation to Future**

Evidence 5: **De-Emphasis on Classroom Work**

Feature 6-n: **Emphasis on Male Domination**

Figure 6: Parallel between Lexical Features and Evidence. The thesis and supports can be represented as shown. The thesis is presented as the New Idea--*Football Should be Banned.* The evidence is summarized in subheads that could be placed directly into the term paper. (Please notice that all subheads of evidence are presented as parallel nouns. Parallel verbs could be used: however, nouns and verbs are not parallel and cannot be used in the same list.)

Chapter 15:
Developing the Thesis

Several years ago, I wrote a paper that was entitled "Remarks on the Thesis." I find that it is precisely appropriate for discussion in this section on the thesis statement. The language is so simple that you will probably think that nothing has been said. If you do, then you should stay far away from a game called "Three-Card Monte." The operator of this game moves a small ball slowly from one shell on a table to another on top of an old cardboard box. At first, he requires that you bet $5 that you can say where the shell is. Of course, you are successful and he gives you $5. This gets you interested. He moves the ball around slowly again and asks for bets of $10. Of course, you are successful once again. Then, he asks for bets of $40. You are confident in yourself and nervously reach for your wallet and do not want others to see how much money you have. You are distracted. The operator can read you like a book. He handles the ball much more rapidly. Slightly confused, you guess. You are wrong and have to give the operator $40.

Then he asks you if you want to play again and get your money back. You say yes. He asks for a bet of $80. You want to get your money back and agree. You lose again. The next bet is for $160. By now you are very nervous but you desperately want one more chance to get your money back. Before long, you have lost more than $300 and want to cry. The operator says that the police are coming and takes his ball and shells and runs off. You do cry. Accordingly, you will pay close attention to "Remarks on the Thesis" and not let Dr. Coreil fool you. Do you see a relationship between the words "Three-Card Monte" and Jeffries' notion of "race"?

Remarks on the Thesis
by Clyde Coreil

If I put a pot of water on a fire, the water will get hot. If I put coins into a certain machine, candy will come out. There is a definite relationship between *fire* and *hot water*, and between *coins* and *candy*. If I see a relationship between two or more things, and if I describe that relationship for the first time, I am probably making a thesis. In my thesis, I am proposing an explanation of how the incidents are related.

Often, we do not even think of such relationships when we do one thing to cause another. If, however, we expect one result and get another, we stop and ask "Why?" For instance, if I push the light switch in the kitchen and water starts running from a faucet, I will call a plumber and an electrician to find out what is wrong. Perhaps the light switch was connected by mistake to the water pump, in which case there was a definite relationship between the switch and the flowing water. Or perhaps the switch and the flowing of water were coincidence. One just happened to take place at the same time as the other. There is no relationship between the two.

Let us take another example. On the average, people in the United States live to be 75 years old. But in one small town, Smithville, most men and women live to be 100. I might well ask, "Why?" What accounts for the difference? What do the residents of Smithville do that others in the U.S.A. fail to do? I might investigate the Smithvillians' diet, their working habits, their personal relationships, and anything else that I can think of to answer the question, "Why do Smithvillians live longer than other Americans?"

One day, I visit the small town and notice that the local residents take short naps at 10 a.m., at 1 p.m. and at 5 p.m. in addition to their normal sleep at night. This pattern of naps is the only difference I can determine between Smithvillians and other Americans. So, I come up with the following explanation for long life: "It seems that short naps during the day can extend the life span of human beings." This is a thesis. Or, more correctly, it is only a hypothesis at this point. It will become a full-fledged thesis only if I explore sleeping and lifespan in other ways and find a positive relationship.

For instance, I can visit the library and read books and articles about sleeping. Perhaps, I will learn that sleep is related to a lowering of stress. Then I read about stress and find out that it can cause high blood pressure. I read about high blood pressure and learn that it can result in kidney disease and fatal strokes. Then I interview a doctor in Smithville and ask is the blood pressure of the people in that town lower or higher than the national average. If I found out that it is very much lower, my hypothesis is on its way to becoming a thesis. If I do additional research and everything points to a relationship between taking naps and low blood pressure, and between low blood pressure and life expectancy, then I will be satisfied that my hypothesis is probably valid.

I will then write a term paper, stating the thesis—"Short naps during the day seem to be fairly closely related to an extended human lifespan"—presenting the evidence that I have found, and saying exactly where I have found it. That is, I will give the titles and page numbers of the books and articles that I have read, and the name of the doctor in Smithville who I interviewed. Probably I will have recorded the interview and will be able to quote him exactly. Perhaps I got some of my information on the radio or television, in which case I will state the title of the program, the name of the station that broadcast it, and the time and date of that broadcast. After all this is done, I will submit my paper to the teacher who will smile and give me a big fat "A" for the course.

A More Formal Definition of "Thesis"

We can now offer a definition of "thesis statement" in slightly more formal terms: *A thesis is the statement of a newly perceived relationship between two or more things supported by objective evidence.* The thesis is the central point around which practically all research is conducted. That certainly includes research on your term paper. A good thesis will guide your selection of books and articles in magazines and newspapers. But there is a catch—it is impossible to make a good thesis statement before you know something about a particular topic. So, on what basis can you select material to read?

One partial solution to this problem is asking the right question. Why would that help? Because a question is usually more general than a thesis. That is, to ask a question, you do not have to know the answer. To make a thesis, on the other hand, you must have at least one answer because that is what a thesis is—an answer to a question. A good question as well as a good thesis can help you select useful articles and books. We have already given an example of such a question: "Why do Smithvillians live longer than other Americans?" If, in your reading, you find that you cannot answer the question exactly as asked, then you are perfectly free to modify that question in order for your thesis answer to fit. Usually, that is what happens to both questions and thesis. They are modified as the research progresses.

Checklist for a Good Thesis

In determining whether or not you have a good thesis, there are several checks you can make. The first involves "objectivity," which is considered the opposite of "subjectivity." A support is objective if it does not rely on personal feelings about something. A subjective support, on the other hand, is based on personal responses or opinions. To better understand these two terms, it is helpful to consider the difference between a *personal essay* and a *research paper*. Both of these types of writing usually have a thesis. The difference is that supports in a research paper can only be objective; in a personal essay, supports can be either objective or subjective.

For example, an acceptable thesis for a personal essay might be the following: "Baseball is a dull game." One support for this relationship between *baseball* and *dull* could be the recollection that you always get bored and start reading a novel when a baseball game comes onto the television screen. Another support is that you find it stupid for anyone to get excited about grown men hitting a ball with a big stick. For a personal essay, such opinions make good supports. For a research paper, however your opinions are not acceptable as supporting evidence. How about the thesis that "Baseball is a dull game"? For a research paper, that thesis is worthless. Why? Because it is a statement of personal opinion. It is subjective in nature.

A far better thesis for a term paper is this: "Despite the fact that baseball is considered the most American of sports, most Americans don't like it." You could support this thesis--assuming that it is accurate—with objective information. You could find out approximately how many of them like baseball. You could never find out exactly how many there are in each group, but you should not let that bother you. Approximate numbers are quite satisfactory.

There are many objective ways of determining these approximate numbers. For instance, you might be able to find surveys in which other researchers have asked various people who make up a representative sample of the population whether or not they like baseball. Also, you might find studies of the sales of baseball-related items such as uniforms, bats, balls and books. You could compare the ratings of TV broadcasts of baseball games to the ratings of more popular TV programs. You could read popular magazines like *People* and compare the number of articles on baseball players to the number of articles on movie stars, politicians, and businessmen. This kind of information is objective: it does not come from your personal feelings about baseball. Rather, it comes from publications in the library, from the expert measurements of authorities in various fields, and possibly from your own careful observations of people, events and situations.

Objectivity: Crucial and Critical

Objectivity, then, is a very important criterion for determining whether a particular statement is good thesis. Another critical criterion is that the thesis must present *new ideas* about relationships. Another way of saying this is that statements of popular, well-accepted beliefs make a very weak thesis. For example, "Computers are essential tools in science and industry." "Seventy years ago, this might have been a very good thesis. Now, it is awful. Why? Because everyone knows it. It is an obvious truth. Other statements that do not make good thesis for the same reason are: "Many children like candy," "Young men tend to be attracted to young women," "Faulty brakes are dangerous," and "Most students get nervous before exams."

This is not to say that a good thesis about popular beliefs cannot be written. The key point is that the relationships must be newly perceived. The reversal of popular beliefs usually entails such perceptions. For example, it is a popular belief that computers are helpful. The idea that computers are harmful is the reversal of that belief. Accordingly, the following thesis is interesting: "Computers hurt more people than they help." If you can support this with objective information from the library and possibly interviews with authorities such as teachers, businessmen and physicians, then your paper will probably be very good,

A good thesis certainly does not have to involve a popular belief. Consider, for instance, this thesis: "Eating certain vegetables can significantly improve a person's score on an I.Q. test." There are probably few people in the world who hold a belief about a positive relationship between vegetables and Intelligence Quotient Scores. Yet a very interesting paper might be written around such a thesis—if the writer can find evidence to support the idea.

It has recently occurred to me that a "Wisdom Quotient" might be a very interesting topic for an Academic Research Paper. I would have to check the internet, the library, and various indexes, and ask professors of psychology if they had heard of such a measurement or anything related to a "W.Q." If I encounter little or no research on this topic, I would be encouraged to pursue it. I would have to be very careful about not making claims that I cannot support. Academia is not a place that tolerates hunches presented as theories that are to be taken seriously. (Incidentally, I found a number of articles on the Wisdom Quotient. Possibly, I could still write a term paper involving the Wisdom Quotient, but I would have to modify my hypothesis.)

The Importance of a Verb

A third way to test for a good thesis is simply to ask if the thesis statement is a complete sentence. Usually, this means, "Does the thesis sentence have a verb?" If it does, you're in good shape. If it doesn't, then you're in trouble. For example, the following is neither a complete sentence nor a thesis statement: "*Population problems and the Hong Kong economy in the next ten years." Not only is there no verb in the preceding stretch of words, there is no clear idea. Am I referring to decreases or increases in the population? The following is an improvement: "Over-population problems could destroy the Hong Kong economy in the next ten years."

A fourth criterion is that a thesis is always a statement and never a question. For example, consider the following: "How can pets destroy families?" It has a verb—*can destroy*--and is grammatically a complete sentence. But it is most definitely not a thesis. To have thesis, you must look for the <u>answer</u> to the question. One such answer is the following: "Pets can destroy families by demanding and receiving from parents the attention and affection that should be given to children." This is a good thesis statement. It presents an answer to the following question: "Can pets destroy families?" It also summarizes the method by which pets can be destructive.

We can summarize the points made so far in this paper by saying that a thesis is an explanation of relationships between two or more things. We noted that that explanation should have the following characteristics:

1. **It must be recently perceived.**
2. **It must be supportable by objective evidence.**
3. **It must contain a verb.**
4. **It must not be a question.**

Complete Originality is not Essential

It is excellent for you to develop a completely original thesis and find evidence to support it. For example, you might read the story of Cinderella and think that it is really about a particular political conflict. You might explain that the glass slipper in the story represented a particular piece of land. The girl named Cinderella represented a poor country that needed this piece of land. After the land was given, the poor country had difficulty in governing it. And so on. You would have to prove that the author of *Cinderella* knew about this "real" political situation, and you would have to show that the other characters in the story represented different influences on that situation. It is very likely that such a thesis has never been made. It is highly original. Many people might be skeptical, but if enough evidence is presented, an original thesis can be the center of a very good term paper.

It is not necessary, however, that the basic thesis be completely original. Another very acceptable type of thesis brings together similar points of view of various authorities writing about the same thing. The element of the new is in the fact that there are many articles coming out that maintain similar points of view. For example, that diet soda is harmful to health. Another example is that in reading recent articles on Shakespeare, you find that several of the authors claim that Shakespeare's plays were really about revolution. Those articles would themselves be evidence for a thesis like the following: "Recently, many scholars have held that running through Shakespeare's plays are his thoughts on the necessity of periodic revolutions in all countries." Again, your evidence would consist of the stated opinions of scholars and of the evidence that they found and presented. If you write such a paper, it is very important to give the names of each scholar, the titles of the articles they wrote, and the magazines that published those articles. If you use the opinion of a scholar and the evidence he presents but do not give him or her credit, then you have committed plagiarism. You have stolen the ideas. That is a very serious offence in college writing.

Let us consider another example of a research paper that uses ideas that are not original with the student-writer. Imagine that you are interested in doing a term paper on Ernest Hemingway, who wrote novels in the first half of the twentieth century. You might start with a question like, "How are the values of life in the United States reflected in the writings of Hemingway?" The values you will concentrate on are individualism, courage and integrity. After choosing this topic, you go to the library and read literary, psychology and sociology magazine articles. In them, you find that these particular values are no longer held in high regard by most Americans. Your initial assumptions must be modified, but you could still write a very interesting paper with this thesis: "The writings of Hemingway reflect certain values of his society, values that are no longer held in high regard in America."

Your term paper will not be weakened by the fact that it was not you but the magazine writers who originated the idea about the relationship between certain values and Americans. You will still be dealing with the strength of the newly perceived relationships. You will be pointing out that many authorities now hold this opinion. Of course, it is extremely important that you report each observation of the magazine writers accurately, that you give the name of the writers, and that you fully document the articles in which their observations were made.

The Importance of Sticking to the Thesis

Before we leave this paper on Ernest Hemingway, we will consider the importance of paying close attention to each part of the thesis because that **thesis is actually the outline on which your term paper will be written**. You should constantly re-read your thesis and make certain that the paper you are writing is in accord with it. In other words, you should explain and support all of the major ideas that are in each part of the thesis, and you should not explain and develop ideas that are not in that thesis.

For example, my thesis might be this: "The eating of certain vegetables can result in higher I.Q. scores." I will be concerned with (1) identifying the vegetables, (2) presenting evidence that the scores of people who ate these vegetables did actually improve, and (3) showing that there is a definite, direct relation between these vegetables and higher I.Q. scores. I will be in serious trouble if I spend half of my paper telling the reader how to cook these foods so that they will taste good, or if I neglect to support any of the three main parts of my thesis.

Let's get back to the Hemingway thesis, which is, "The writings of Hemingway reflect certain values of his society, values that are no longer held in America." According to the Hemingway thesis, there are three main parts clearly reflected in Hemingway's writing:

1. **Hemingway's writings consistently reflected certain values.**
2. **These values were held in high regard by Americans who were living when Hemingway was writing,**
3. **These values are no longer held by Americas who are living now.**

This three-part thesis would probably result in a paper that is longer than the one required by the instructor. By eliminating one of the three parts above, you would simplify your thesis and shorten your paper. For example, if you eliminate Part Number One, your thesis will be something like this: "In the middle of the Twentieth Century, many Americans stopped believing in individualism, courage and integrity." Of course, your paper would no longer be concerned with Hemingway, but it could still be a good work.

If you eliminate Part Number Two and keep Parts One and Three, your thesis would be: "The values in Hemingway's writings are not held in high regard by most contemporary Americans." You would no longer be primarily interested in showing that Hemingway's values were the values of his time and society. If you eliminate Part Number Three but keep Parts One and Two, your thesis will probably be: "The values in Hemingway's writings were the values held in high regard by his society." Here, you would not be concerned with the loss of those values in contemporary America.

The main point in discussing these eliminations is to illustrate the possibility that you can control your paper by controlling the thesis. Every time you sit down to work on your paper, you must ask yourself, "Am I sticking to the thesis? If not, why not?" You might find that you have to eliminate part of the thesis. On the other hand, you might find that you have to eliminate part of the paper. If so, do so. The balance between thesis and development is crucial. When you are done with assembling the title, the introductory material, the presentation of background, the discussion of each piece of evidence, the conclusion which might well make reference to the material presented in the very first sentence of the term paper, and the Works Cited, your whole project should seem the presentation of a single, small, original topic. If it seems effortless and natural, you will have done your job well. Both you and I will know quite well that it was not effortless but was the product of many hours of hard work. You should make a very clean printout for yourself in addition to the one you hand in. You will have this original as reference when you are asked by another professor to write a term paper. If so, tell her or him that you will use the present term paper as a model for the execution of the second paper. Offer to let him see this paper so he will understand that you wrote it yourself and that you did not purchase it online.

A Final Checklist

Considering the importance of sticking to the thesis, we might add it to our checklist and repeat our definition of a thesis. A thesis is an explanation of relationships between two or more things. That explanation should have the following characteristics:

1. **It must be recently perceived,**
2. **It must be supportable by objective evidence,**
3. **It must not affirm a popular belief,**
4. **It must contain a verb,**
5. **It must not be a question,**
6. **It must be in agreement with the development of ideas in the paper.**

Conclusion

Making a hypothesis is something we all do practically everyday of our lives. If we insert a dollar bill into a change machine, and the dollar is rejected, we examine it to make certain that it is not folded. That is, we make a thesis: "The dollar bill was rejected because it was folded. If I flatten it out, the machine will probably accept it and belch out coins." The first thesis relating heat and a pot of water was made a very long time ago. Since then, scientists have formalized their ideas into a thesis countless times. As the saying goes, "There's nothing new under the sun." Nothing–except the discovery and perception of relationships

***

Chapter 16:
Developing a Term Paper Topic

It is crucial that two points be considered as you are beginning to develop a topic for your term paper. First, you should not choose a topic about which you hold a definite, unchangeable point of view. If you do, the evidence you present will likely be biased. You will very likely ignore any information that does not support your point of view, and you will present only information that does. This is very near the essence of propaganda, and not the honest seeking for the truth that is in accord with academia. Second, your opinion should be the result of the best, most objective evidence you can find and discuss. It is perfectly acceptable to make small changes in your title or even to adopt a point of view that is in direct opposition to the one you started out with. That is part of the process of Academic Writing.

In other words, you should not begin working on a term paper topic if you are already convinced that you are right. An essential part of the process of writing a term paper is searching for truth. At the very least, you must be ready and willing to change your opinion if such a change is indicated by the evidence. This requires your setting the bar very high. You have taken the first steps of that height by your decision to come to the university. If your main concern was in equipping yourself for job, then you must realize that all jobs entail principled responsibility. You can help develop in yourself the moral fiber you will need to make responsible decisions. One of the many ways you can do this is by your attitude towards your studies. And the principles of term paper topic development are in accord with that moral fiber and principled responsibility.

One of the most effective ways of developing a term paper topic is asking a very small question about something you are very much interested in. For example, if you have a keen interest in still photography, you might ask a question involving the change from film to digital cameras. You know that a few photographers resist that change and continue to use film technology, which is quite different. A question that takes us closer to a term paper topic is: "Why do some photographers resist the change to digital cameras?" One of the primary rules in formulating a title is that it cannot be a question. Since we wish to respect convention, we can turn this question into a title without much difficulty: "Reasons for Resisting the Change from Film to Digital Photography."

One reason for rejecting the latter title is that it exceeds the limit of nine words. This excess is corrected by changing the title to "Resistance to Digital: The Preference for Film Photography." With eight words, we have come in under the limit. In my opinion, this title is satisfactory. It states that the paper will be concerned, not with something broad like comparing digital to film technology, but with resistance to change based on preference that can be verified through research involving, for example, interviews with photographers, articles in magazines, the internet, and any other source of information. The more varied the sources; the stronger the evidence. There are limits to that principle, but it does serves as a good "rule of thumb."

The internet provides a seemingly endless access to articles that relate one topic to another. In writing a term paper, this is an invaluable source of information. It is, however, important that we do not become addicted to the search engine as the only source available to us. There is virtually always a point at which we can take information from the internet and pursue directions of research on our own. In the next chapter, we will mention again the value of calling or e-mailing an agency or office that is related to our topic, which happens to be the relationship between song lyrics and substance abuse. This is a very small area to which the internet led us and provided the names of agencies and university departments concerned with lyrics and drugs.

At this point, we can turn from the search engine and get in touch with those agencies by e-mail or letter, and ask for literature on the topic or even for the list of nearby offices that we might visit for the purpose of conducting an interview. We would, of course, prepare for that interview by making a list of up to ten questions--from which we can vary as necessary during the interview. The important point here is that we can add to the depth and interest of our term papers by putting out the energy needed to pursue topics on our own. We certainly can attempt to offer those papers for publication in a magazine or journal or indeed a website concerned with the relationship between song lyrics and substance abuse.

Practicing for the Real Paper

For your Practice Paper, which is due at the Mid-Term Examination, all of the students will have the same topic: "Banning Football in the Schools." Developing a suitable topic is an important part of your second paper, due one week before the Final Exam. The prime criterion of a suitable topic is whether or not you are interested in it. Surely there is something with which you have been involved in elementary or secondary school. For instance, your teacher might have asked you to help in caring for a certain plant. You did so out of a sense of duty at first, then you came to enjoy it. It seemed every now and then that there was some communication between you and the plant. The possibility of that communication might indeed make an excellent topic for your term paper.

You could go to your search engine and enter these words: "Have any studies been done on the possible communication between human beings and plants?" Or you can make it shorter: "Communication between humans and plants." You might have to alter your topic to "Communication between plants." If you have an interest in communication and plants, you are almost home. Just keep tweaking that topic until you have something with which you can begin to work. At that point, the term paper will cease being a pain and become an avid interest that is much stronger than before.

Unfortunately, this type of search engine entry often results in information on a topic that someone has considered before. But practically always, you can take a slightly different approach. Or, you can look ask the Genie in the Search Engine about experiments done on plants that involve communication. Or you can call up "Roses and Sunshine." Your computer will not fail to find in its vast repertoire of publications a lead that you can pursue.

I suggest that you do not take "capital punishment" or "abortion" as your topic because thousands of papers have been written on them. It is difficult to find something new to say about these topics. You should also be careful of asking a question like: "How has the international attitude towards abortion changed during the past 100 years?" You would need a paper of some 350 pages to do justice to that question. I repeat: the term paper should be concerned with the precise and narrow development of the topic you have outlined in the title. For example, you might consider whether mothers sometimes identify too closely with their daughters in high school competitions.

Or, if you are a biology major, you might consider whether a relationship between sleep and the formation of bone has been reported in several journal articles. Or you can edge back into moral seriousness with a review of contemporary reactions to the "armed drone" which the United States has been using as an alternate to "boots on the ground," that is to having soldiers go into various countries to oppose the policies of certain groups. You will not present this simply as a review but as an argument in favor of the drones or against them. One of the major advantages of such narrow topics is that the number of sources that deal with them is very likely far more limited. This is good because you can gain a certain amount of mastery over this information, which will lead to an informed point of view.

Approximating Gutenberg

This leads me to suggest seriously that the search engine on your computer is the most powerful and significant development in the management of information since the invention of movable type in approximately 1439 by Johannes Gutenberg. Very rarely do I find that the computer cannot suggest an answer in terms of articles in which the question has been considered. Having access to this enormous power opens many possibilities, that in turn become responsibilities to the class-work you do and to yourself. I say this because this is a very special time in your life. Every day, you will meet someone or be involved in an interesting class, or chat with a professor who knows very well several of the hundreds of things you can do to enrich your life. Perhaps it would be feasible for you to combine these chance encounters, and maybe even select a topic that has arisen in conversation with these persons. What you must be absolutely certain of from the beginning is that you have access to specific evidence and not just to your memory of how things were in another country. The presence of a central thesis and of specific, pointed evidence is always of primary importance.

Buying Ready-Made Term Papers on the Internet

It is possible to find the addresses of companies that keep thousands of term papers on file. For a price, they will choose one upon request and maybe for an additional price, they will change the paper a bit so that your professor might accept it as work done by you for his or her class. For customers able to pay hundreds of dollars for a custom-made term paper, they will even write original versions. Do not even consider this. It is plagiarism of a very low kind. If I find evidence that you have chosen to do this in my class, I will begin an investigation and, if warranted, report it to the Dean and to the Grievance Committee of the University Senate that deals with matters of this sort. I will personally testify before any body that might be convened about this grievous offense.

I have spent countless hours preparing this book on academic term papers and composition, mainly to use with you. I am no different from other teachers, virtually all of whom consider your outperforming them in a particular field the greatest of compliments they could receive. Those other professors are at least equally involved in preparations they make for class. It would be truly shameful for you to do something like attempt to buy another student's term paper and present it to your classmates and to me as your own. It could also have consequences explored in Chapter 10: Plagiarism, Theft and Term Papers. Believe me, this is scurrilous behavior which is forbidden in our society.

###

Chapter 17:
Organization: Broad Principles

In Chapter 8: Naming the Categories, we discussed the great importance of balance between categories and features. I advise you to read that chapter again before you proceed with this one. In Chapter 11: Rubrics and Evaluation, we considered closely the first category of evaluation via rubric, which concentrated on "Content." I would like to turn now to the second category, "Organization." Let us look at the remarks that would get a "Poor" rating: **"Writing is rambling and unfocused, with main thesis and supporting details presented in a disorganized, unrelated way."** "Rambling" means moving here and there with no real direction. "Unfocused" means presented without clear borders marking the edges of thoughts, concepts and sentences. If we enumerate or give numbers to the constituents of something, we will have been attempting to focus both ourselves and the reader on the matter at hand.

Personally, I think that everything concerning organization is as much for the writer as for the reader. For me, writing is more than an attempt to <u>express</u> how I feel about something: it is rather an attempt to <u>find out</u> how I feel about it. At times, my position on a particular topic changes during and/or after the time I have spent writing about it. So that organization helps not only the reader and the evaluator, it helps me bring my thoughts together and formulate a point that I can make in writing. I write a lot in different genres such as the short story, the drama, and exposition—as I am doing here. I usually carry a notebook with me at all times. If I get an idea, I have to note it or I forget it. My writing and my thinking are intertwined. I suggest that you get a small notebook and a pen for jotting down your thoughts during the day. Once you begin, it will get easier. And you will inevitably find that this system of notation is part of your thinking. Sometimes when I am checking attendance, I will ask you if you have your "Small Notebook" with you. If you do, I will be favorably impressed.

Organization and the Rubric

These are the remarks for a rating of "Acceptable" on the rubric. **"Writing demonstrates some grasp of organization, with a discernible thesis and supporting details."** "Discernible" means that we can recognize it. In this book, we have referred to "supporting details" as the categories of evidence and the elements that make up the categories. The remarks in the rubric for a rating of "Excellent" are as follows: **"Writing is clearly organized around a central thesis. Each paragraph is clear and relates to the others in a well-planned framework."**

On the "macro-level," this "well-planned framework" refers to the overall organization in your paper. On the "micro-level," it refers to the relationship between any given sentence and the preceding sentence. More precisely, each sentence in a paragraph is based on one word or phrase in the preceding sentence or part of that sentence. In other words, the clarity of a paragraph results from the expansion of one specific word or idea in one sentence being developed in the words that follow. I exemplify this in Figure 7 below. When one sentence no longer develops from a word or idea in the previous sentence, it is time to begin a new paragraph. Please check the writing in one of your other textbooks. You will find that this is a simple but well used technique.

Another time you should think about beginning a new paragraph is when the one you are writing has reached a maximum of approximately 120 words. If you do not do so, your readers will begin to think that they are in the middle of a wide river of words. They will be less and less interested in a close understanding of your ideas. Their primary concern is simply to look briefly at each of the words between him and the other shore. You should help the reader with his or her task by choosing a breaking point and beginning a new paragraph. The indentation at the beginning of the line and its relationship to a natural shift in topic will provide your reader a chance to rest for a moment. Occasionally, a minor subhead will be most welcome. For example, if you are describing two automobiles, arrange the descriptions in two paragraph--if the single paragraph you are writing is reaching 120 words.

Graphic Design

The opposite is also true: try to never begin a new paragraph after you have written less than 50 words. Once in a while, this is acceptable. But as a frequently occurring structure, this is not good. If you have to change things around, then do so. We can summarize this by saying that graphic design plays a very important role in the appearance and degree of understanding of a printed page. I invite you: open any of your other textbooks to any page, and you will find evidence of a graphic designer attempting to make that page interesting. He or she most definitely will avoid having the mass of words constitute a "wide river." Now, a second invitation: Open a scholarly journal, and you will probably not find evidence of a graphic designer at work. Journals are usually edited by persons who are expert in their field of molecular biology or nanotechnology, and not in graphic design. In fact, many of these experts would be embarrassed by the idea of applying graphic design to their copy.

****

Figure 7. Lexical Source of Continuity in Paragraph Structure. Each sentence in a paragraph is based on one word or phrase in the preceding sentence or part of that sentence. For example in the following, "home" and "house" refer to similar elements and both have number "1" under them.

Sam went <u>home</u> at 6 p.m. His <u>house</u> was <u>old and looked awful</u>, but it <u>sheltered</u>
        1   1   2   2
his <u>family</u>. His <u>wife and three children</u> were the <u>center</u> of his universe. He
    3   3   3
<u>liked</u> his job, but he <u>loved</u> these <u>four human beings</u> far more than even he
  4   4   3
could have imagined <u>before he got married</u>. <u>Then,</u> he was concerned mainly
                      5   5
with <u>himself</u>. He wouldn't for a moment choose to return to <u>single life</u>.
  6   6

****

Transition Words

Another principle that is fundamental to organization is that the sense of the underlying meaning is critical in any piece of writing. Expressions of the relationships of place to elements, of direction to sequence, of cause to effect—these are performed by little words like "because;" "first" followed by "second" and "third;" "do so" and "so do"—the number of these words is enormous. However, if the reader is to be taken by the hand, they must be mastered and used, particularly in formal, academic writing. For example, in Figure 7, <u>old and looked awful</u> needs to be differentiated from <u>sheltered</u>. The former idea is negative; the latter, positive. Therefore, we use <u>but</u>, which warns the reader that the basic ideas are different. Although they may be small, underlying differences are important, and the reader should always know where he or she is going.

On the next page, there is presented a "Skeletal Outline" of a term paper and the length in words of the various sections of that piece of writing. I present these separately from the text so that you might recognize them more easily.

***

<u>SKELETAL OUTLINE FOLLOWS ON NEXT PAGE</u>

****

Figure 8. Skeletal Outline of Academic Paper: On the next page, there are several units of information. The first is an Outline which provides the various sections of a term paper. The first four are followed by Roman Numerals, a conventional method of indicating that that particular page is not part of the presentation of the argument of the paper . The second nine are the numbered parts of the sections we have already studied: Introduction, Background, Evidence and Conclusion. Following the Outline is an approximation of the proper length of each section expressed in words. The small Roman numerals after "Title, Bio-Blurb, and Abstract" indicate that the main part of the text has not yet begun. Arabic numbers indicate the text has begun.

Skeletal Outline of Academic Paper

TITLE and AUTHOR... i

BIO-BLURB.................. ii (Note on the Author)

ABSTRACT iii

INTRODUCTION——— **1. Old Idea**
2. New Idea
3. Naming of Categories of Evidence

BACKGROUND——— **4. Background**

EVIDENCE——————— **5. Discussion of 1st Category of Evidence**
6. Discussion of 2nd Category of Evidence
7. Discussion of 3rd Category of Evidence
8. Discussion of 4th Category of Evidence

CONCLUSION——— **9. Conclusion**

(Limited Option .... **Extend slightly whatever you choose)**

Length in Words of Various Sections of Term Paper

The length of each of the four above sections is definite but flexible. You can make any of the sections a little longer or shorter than called for in the formula below:

Title: Maximum of 9 words

Bio-Blurb: 1/20 of total words

Abstract: 1/20 of total words

Introduction: 4/20 of total words (Quotations do not count.)

Background: /20 of total words

Evidence: 11/20 of total words

Conclusion: 1/20 of total words

****

Abstract

We have not yet mentioned the "abstract," which many journals require and which is printed above the article or paper itself. Because it is a part of much professional writing, we will include it in this book. The abstract should not be written until the paper is 100% complete. At that point, you should summarize all of the contents of the paper and print them under the heading "Abstract." The abstract will be placed before any part of the paper, except the title and information on the author—above quite irreverently called a "Bio-Blurb," more formally, "Note on the Author." Draw a heavy line under the abstract to indicate that it is not part of the actual paper.

In Figure 9, you will notice that we have centered 14-point Times New Roman font for the title: "Unseen Dangers in High School Sports," followed by the word "by" and the name of the author in 12-point font. In my educated opinion, this specification results in graphic balance. You will also notice that the Note on the Author is printed in italics to make it clear that it is not part of the paper itself. The biographical sketch should be at least 20 words in length and no more than 50. Do not estimate: count the words.

****

Figure 9. Example of the 'Title, Author, Bio-Blurb, Abstract' with which we will begin our papers. The "Bio-Blurb'" is printed in italics to indicate that it is not part of the paper itself.

Football:
A Sport Whose Time Has Come and Gone
by
Gerald Cobbler

Note on the Author

Gerald Cobbler is a sophomore at New Jersey City University in Jersey City, NJ. Although he has not officially chosen a major, he leans heavily toward Criminal Justice and law school after he graduates. More precisely, he is interested in working with juvenile offenders and has written several term papers on that subject.

Abstract

The belief that danger is a necessary part of growing up for males between the ages of 13 and 19 seems to result from an accurate assessment of maturation. However, the sport of football dramatically increases the chances that there will occur a debilitating injury of a physical or moral nature.

Introduction

****
***

Cognitive Awareness

If you follow this pattern of presentation of elements, your paper should be fairly well organized. There is one aspect of organization that we have not mentioned--"Cognitive Awareness," which means thinking about thinking. Here, we are perhaps more concerned with "talking about writing" while we are writing. We can think of taking a reader by the hand and telling him exactly what we are doing as we do it. This is an excellent way of proceeding. It is closely related to the use of the "Editorial We."

Personal pronouns--such as "I, you, they"--are of course not used by the writer in the paper itself. Here, "we" is not really a personal pronoun but a way of identifying with the paper itself. For example: "We will explore this hypothesis by considering four categories related to form: (1) size, (2) shape, (3) color, and (4) weight." In the preceding sentence, "we" does not refer to persons but to the writer who is using a <u>well accepted convention</u>. The writer never says, "*I will consider the categories." That is outside the convention and would mark the writer as an amateur and definitely would not be acceptable in graduate school. However, this "we" does give the writer permission to guide the reader through concepts that might otherwise be difficult to understand.

Separate Outlines

It is appropriate that we mention here the "outline" that is often required on a separate page preceding the text. What we have done is taken that outline and inserted it into the term paper itself. Personally, I find that this makes the outline--as well as the term paper--more dynamic. If you are more comfortable with the separate outline, then by all means go through the paper and note the title, the thesis statement, the subheads, and the minor subheads. You may arrange these--except the thesis statement--into either all sentences or all parallel noun phrases or verb phrases. Do not attempt to form questions out of these phrases, as that is considered to interfere with consistency. It is important, however, that you not extract anything from the text: to do so would be to lose the marks of organization that has occupied us thus far. In other words, you can add an outline but do not attempt to delete a subhead, explaining that the subhead is now in the outline.

It is also important that we do not forget the main points of outlining, which is usually a matter of dividing a central entity into equal parts of diminishing importance. As a first example, let us call our central entity the HEAD. It is at the highest level of this way of arranging subdivisions. Although there is no limit to the major divisions of the HEAD, we usually find between three and nine. The major divisions are indicated by Roman Numerals (I, II, III, IV, V, VI, VII, VIII, IX, X and so on). It is of considerable importance that if we divide one of these, we must have at least two parts. In other words, we cannot have a single "A" under III. Proverbial wisdom tells us that a single "A" should be incorporated into III. This is not to say that all divisions must have an equal number of parts: all divisions, rather, must have least two parts.

If we wish to divide "A," we use Arabic numbers: 1,2,3,4, and so on. If we wish to make an even smaller division, we can use small Roman letters: a, b, c, d, and so on. Each small division should be indented about three spaces. We attempt to illustrate these relationships as in Figure 10.

****

Figure 10: Note on Outlining. The "Head" of an outline is the name of the item (title) that is being divided. The names of the first divisions or categories is "Subhead A," "Subhead B," "Subhead C" and so on. If there is no "B" but only "A," we must combine the Head with the single Subhead. This is often done by using a colon (":") after the Head. For example: "The Vietnam War: An Era of Errors."

HEAD		GRAIN
A.		A. Food for Humans
	1.	1. Bread
	2.	2. Vegetables
B.		B. Industry
	1.	1. Farms
	2.	2. Gasoline Substitute
C.		C. Research Topic
	1.	1. University Labs
		a.	a. Genetic Variations
		b.	b. Graduate Study
	2.	2. Private Business
		a.	a. Economical Production
		b.	b. Ecological Effects
		c.	c. Sales and Advertising

****

Chapter 18:
Application of Organizational Principles

A term paper entitled "Evil in Macbeth" is doomed to failure. The topic is hopelessly broad and pretentious, even for a 350-page dissertation. In Chapter 16, we saw that an incomparably more realistic and promising a topic can be developed by asking and answering a limited question about a limited subject. In this chapter, we will consider 70 specific questions that might well lead to balanced term papers. Questions are virtually always broader than answers, and the ones below are no exception. One of the advantages of limited questions is that we can usually see what is the situation with regard to the developments in the area of our initial question. If we like what we see, we can call up the indicated references immediately. If we find that variation might yield a better result for our term paper, we can easily make a variation in the search engine such as Google.

What we are doing is trying to coax the search engine to give us information that fits the parameters of the paper we have been describing. However, our search for information we wish to use for one purpose will almost certainly teach us techniques of using the search engine and the enormous store of information categorically organized in the internet. In other words, our work on the term paper results in our learning to locate and call up more and more specialized information on a given topic.

For example, we might ask **Item #32** from the list below. That question is:

How is music being used in the treatment of drug addiction?

Since Item #32 is relatively short, the simple first step is to type it directly into the search engine. I did this in reality and seven of the first 14 sites given dealt with music and treatment of drug addiction problems. I selected the most interesting sites and printed them out. As a basis for this selection, I used the mention of "allows, clients to explore their feelings about being unable to control their use of harmful substances" that was provided in the brief description of the site. I opened this site, read the material, liked the element of "feelings" or "emotions" and printed it out. There were about 20 sections dealing with music therapy, including the section on "Substance Abuse." I print out part of that section below:

> Music therapy activities involving emotional exploration, such as music listening and discussion, lyric analysis and songwriting are particularly effective toward this end. Purdon-Ostertag (1986), in working with drug-dependent individuals who were particularly negative and complained of feelings of boredom or "nothing," found that improvisation on these themes revealed quite concrete feelings.' The music expressed anger, sadness, a sense of longing, disappointment and frustration. In the discussion and sharing that followed the improvisation the clients were able to acknowledge the existence of these feelings, differentiate between them, and explore them further.

From Substance Abuse in the Music
Therapy Association of British Columbia

I was interested in pursuing "lyric analysis" which deals with lyrics which are the words in a song. After printing out the Substance Abuse section from which I found the complete electronic address of the site, I altered my inquiry in the search engine to the following:

Lyric analysis in substance abuse music therapy. I got 11 "hits," several of which dealt with lyric analysis. I print out the first two below:

Search Results

The use of <u>music therapy</u> with <u>substance abusers</u> - Title here!
www.wfmt.info/Musictherapyworld/modules/.../showarticle.php?...17...
The use of **music therapy** with **substance abusers** ... Conclusions showed the use of **lyric analysis** and song sharing was particularly useful for enabling residents ...
[PDF]

<u>Music Therapy</u> in <u>Substance Abuse</u> Treatment - American Music ...
www.musictherapy.org/assets/1/7/bib_substanceabuse.pdf
File Format: **PDF**/Adobe Acrobat - Quick View
Trauma, Depression, & **Substance Abuse**: Selected References and Key Findings. STATEMENT OF PURPOSE: **Music therapists** commonly serve persons with ...

At this point, I knew that I was interested in lyric analysis in music therapy related to the treatment of substance abuse. After a few more printouts, and I had the name and e-mail address of someone with whom I could discuss the details of how song lyrics could be analyzed to help persons who were suffering from substance abuse. Because I am a university student, I was accorded particularly polite treatment. I had a tentative title:

Analysis of Song Lyrics: Aiding Treatment of Substance Abuse

I had learned that persons suffering from this condition could be guided to an interpretation of the words of selected songs in a way that was especially meaningful and helpful. I read more and made more printouts. It occurred to me even short sentences, phrases and even single words in certain contexts can have a powerful effect on the human mind. I made notes on this and on the relation that quite likely exists between language, mental illness, and therapy. I made an additional note that I was to check this out on the internet at a later time. After much underlining and notation, I knew the direction in which I was heading. It allowed me to express the old idea that I was replacing.

<u>Old Idea</u>

Normally, the words of a song express an emotion, a feeling about love, loyalty, hate, sorrow, or jealousy that makes that particular song pleasant and possibly amusing in the context of our lives in general.

There is a difference between that general meaning and the sharp relevance that close analysis of that song can hold for some of us in particular. Whereas the song was about a friend who had come to be dear to someone, the close analysis we made with a therapist uncovered a special depth of wealth and significance held by the words interpreted in terms of highly personal situation. The words came to mean more as we thought of them in relation to a particular person who we knew and could name and remember.

The first time we heard that song, we were opening a car door and saw a perfect stranger who we seemed to recognize. Later, we asked someone for the name of that stranger, and one day we ran into him or her by accident. We found that we remembered the clothes they were wearing and the color of their hat. We came to be very close to them. When they were killed in an accident, a part of us seemed to die. The sadness grew into a depression which was so painful that we used more and more drugs to fight it off. We were unable to mention it to anyone, and the drugs became the center of our lives.

Then we went to a therapist who was able to perceive our state of mind. He or she was able to ask the right question at the right time. Slowly, we came to see ways in which the person who had passed reminded us of other persons we had known before. In short, we understood ourselves better and were able to begin to deal with the addiction.

Back to the Term Paper

Finally, after yet more reading and discussing the relation between the close analysis of lyrics and the presence of a particular piece of music, I was able to articulate in one sentence the single idea that I would develop into a term paper. In other words, this was the invaluable "thesis statement" that all academic term papers must have. This sentence would be the center, the glue that contains the heart of the idea for which I would find the supporting evidence. That thesis statement follows:

Thesis Statement
(New Idea)

The close analysis of lyrics and the power of the music in which they are embedded can serve as the source of strength and understanding addicts desperately need in regaining control of their lives.

This would be the new idea, the hypothesis that I would present. When I had read over the articles again and again, I found that the information containing the supporting evidence could be discussed in four categories as follows:

Presentation of Supporting Evidence

We will examine evidence that seems to support our hypothesis in four areas: (1) the comments of the therapists, (2) changes in employment status, (3) purchases of CD's with music, and (4) reported attitudes towards the future.

One of the main reasons why I numbered the pieces of evidence is that I was writing this term paper with the intention of using it as a reference for future assignments in different courses. With the numbers, I would stay away from the narrative but instead continue my search for objective evidence. I continued to narrow and alter my search until I felt that I knew that I could ask more general but relevant questions of persons working in music therapy, law enforcement, and rehabilitation centers. I would prepare for these interviews by writing out up to 10 specific questions related to the areas in which the persons interviewed were working. I would continue to deepen my understanding of the relationship between the analysis of lyrics, music therapy and substance abuse.

The Need for Articulation in a Different Topic

Once we have settled on a possible topic and done the preliminary questioning of the search engine--for example "Google"--we should articulate to ourselves the areas we will be concerned with. The first area I looked into dealt with the "banning" of football as a high school sport. I typed into the search engine this question: "Why should football be banned in secondary and elementary school?" My choice of the word "ban" was interesting but restrictive. To "ban" something implies that it is inherently dangerous. Football is that. But I came across some interesting information that might widen the reasons for cancelling football. Those reasons dealt with "expense"--not only to the school but to the players themselves. I therefore widened the topic of my paper to "Football: A Sport Whose Time Has Passed."

Such interaction between tentative topics and their changing as a result of new information encountered is a well respected part of Academic Writing. Therefore, I modified my topic, which was now concerned with the cancelling of football for reasons in addition to the injuries incurred. Tentatively, I planned to divide my evidence into four categories: (1) injuries, (2) violence, (3) expense, and (4) participation.

I had seen each of these categories arise in one form or other in the course of my reading. I did not find "injuries" discussed in one source; "expense" in another; and "violence" and "participation" in separate articles. However, I did consider it my responsibility to make those divisions myself. In one printout, I would mark one or more sections with a circled (3) and others with a circled (1). When I began to write a first draft, I would naturally collect the circled "1's" and deal with them together in one category--"Injuries." I would deal with the circled "2's" in a second category entitled "Violence." And so on. In this way, I attempted to give my paper the invaluable quality of "coherence."

****

Chapter 19:
Specific Questions to Aid in Developing a Topic

Following are 70 specific questions to be used as beginning points in developing a topic for your term paper. Most of these are asked, not to be answered, but to provide points of departure. If you do not like any of these 70 items, you are welcome to come up with your own, provided that your question has at least two elements, like "communication" between "plants" in Item #1 below. You should consult the procedure described in "Chapter 18: Application of Organizational Principles."

1. Do plants communicate with people? With other plants?
2. Why do some professionals prefer film to digital technology?
3. Why do some people like to collect things?
4. Is there any relation between neglected children and gender?
5. Is there a relation between neglected children and choice of profession?
6. What causes some students to adopt an added role of campus leadership where before there was rebellion?
7. To what extent do some animals help depressed individuals out of their depression?
8. Why are the halls of schools and colleges so often devoid of paintings and other formal decoration?
9. Under what conditions do siblings become violent in their apparent hatred of each other? Is there a relation between children having dogs and cats and their socialization?
10. Is there a relation between children who work outside the home and success in socialization?
11. What is the effect on children of mothers who spend time as prison inmates?
12. What is the relation between being responsible for the care of dogs or cats and the academic performance of those children in school?
13. Can plays be developed that help students of a second language?
14. Has a happiness / sadness index been developed to rank people?
15. Should children be given the responsibility of designing their own bedrooms?
16. Should children be asked to choose a musical instrument and to learn to play it reasonably well?
17. Should children and parents play musical instruments and sing together?
18. What is the relation between mothers and her dreams of the future of the unborn child?
19. What behaviors have an unintended negative effect on racial relations in college?
20. What effect do sports have on children who do not like sports?
22. To what extent has undergraduate college come to be considered little more than a finishing school for poorly performing students in secondary school?
23. Are there any positive alternatives to a college education?

24. To what extent are "food supplements" constituting an alternative to the medicine-control system provided by pharmacies in the USA?

25. Does medical education in the USA include instruction in "food supplements"?

26. What part do firearms play in the identity of young men in rural America?

27. Is color an important element in the treatment of mental disorders in the USA?

28. What innovations have there been in the use of drama to treat mental disorders?

29. Is the construction of three-dimensional structures important to the treatment of mental disorders in the USA?

30. How are animals used in the treatment of mental disorders in the USA?

31. How is music being used in the treatment of mental disorders in the USA?

32. Is music (drama, art, dancing) being used in the treatment of drug addiction?

33. Have there been innovations in the use of music (dance, art, dancing, sewing) in the education of children in the USA?

34. Has the use of "armed drones" changed the ways in which diplomatic relations are conducted between the USA and other countries?

35. Are there any disadvantages to for-profit universities?

36. Should senior citizens be prohibited from working?

37. What are the advantages of salaried employment for teenagers outside the home?

38. Are there innovations in the use of mirrors in design?

39. What are the main negative effects of the internet?

40. To what extent has Alzheimer's Disease been misdiagnosed?

41. What have been the negative effects on students of High Stakes Testing?

42. To what extent has the evaluation of teachers been influenced by High Stakes Testing?

43. Why have private schools resisted High Stakes Testing?

44. What are the advantages of studying Latin in colleges and universities?

45. What have been the negative effects of conceiving of colleges and universities as corporations?

46. To what extent have countries outside the USA conceived of colleges as corporations?

47. To what extent have colleges in the USA been accused of being out of touch with the needs of occupations and professions in the contemporary world?

48. What been the most serious objections to the Occupy Wall Street movement?

49. To what extent have American soldiers returning from Iran and Afghanistan sought to be disassociated from those the conflicts in those countries?

50. To what extent has the American public ignored the service of veterans returning from conflicts in Iraq and Afghanistan?

51. To what extent has the cost of higher education resulted in negative decisions?

52. To what extent has the anti-hero replaced the traditional hero in contemporary literature?

53. What characters in contemporary fiction and drama have emerged as the embodiment of the strengths and virtues of the female in contemporary society?

54. To what extent has the female replaced the male as the embodiment of positive strengths and virtues in contemporary literature?

55. What are the main strengths that characterize the hero in contemporary science fiction?

56. To what extent has the role of Ernest Hemingway as the author and representative hero of his own fiction been duplicated in American fiction?

57. To what extent has the American fighter pilot come to represent the strengths and virtues of the American cowboy as legendary hero in American society?

58. To what extent has wealth replaced the traditional strengths of the American as representing the virtues of freedom, self-reliance and inventiveness?

59. To what extent has the image of the down-trodden underdog replaced the image of the self-reliant, imaginative entrepreneur in the American Dream?

60. To what extent has the image of the hungry, suffering, unrecognized artist emerged in the world of rock music?

61. Has the image of the Byronic Hero been transformed in the arts of America?

62. To what extent has the dual role of President as (1) head of state and (2) dynamic politician evolved in America?

63. To what extent have conflicts ever arisen in the USA between the President as head of the nation and the Governor as head of a state within the nation?

64. What is the relation between recognition and accomplishment in American schools?

65. To what extent does international travel remain an expectation of the well-rounded education of American teenagers?

66. "Mono-lingualism can be cured." To what extent does this statement represent a position of Americans?

67. To what extent have changes in the design and appearance of bicycles reflected the changing identity of American teenagers over the years?

68. To what extent has the motorcycle changed from a means of transportation and become a design motif in itself?

69. To what extent is class a decisive factor in the choice of one's spouse?

70. To what extent does class represent a limit in the promotion of executives similar to the "glass ceiling" that has been recognized as applicable to women?

Your Question, chosen from above list or constructed by you:

71. _____

***

Chapter 20:
Language

The performance classification "Poor" in the part of our rubric entitled "Language" makes reference to several areas, including grammar. Let us look at the exact wording: ***"Writing lacks sentence variety. Significant deficiencies in wording, spelling, grammar, punctuation, or presentation."*** Errors in word choice and grammar cannot be handled in this book: the relevant rules are too many. It is assumed that by the time the student is concerned with term papers, many of these will have been covered in class or learned in everyday conversation. Fortunately, many errors in spelling are caught and sometimes corrected by the computers we all use. However, for reasons that defy logic, very few teachers in the world today address presentation errors in what I call "preformulations." In chapters 1, 2, 29, 30 and 31, I deal with my own personal theory concerning these structures, which have an enormous effect on writing and on the general mastery of any language.

In the category of "Acceptable" language, there is written in the rubric: **"Some sentence variety; adequate usage of wording, grammar, and punctuation."** Under "Excellent," this is written: **"Wide variety of sentence structures. Excellent word usage, spelling, grammar, and punctuation. Effective integration of information."** You will notice that "sentence variety" is mentioned prominently in all three performance classifications: Poor, Acceptable and Excellent. Because it is presented as very important in the rubric, I give some 23 specific variations in sentence structure, and ask the students to consciously and intentionally integrate them in their writing.

It is interesting that "effective integration of information" is found only under "Excellent." Whether or not this is intentional, it gives us a clue as to what is considered an important part of language usage. I deal with the integration of information in the discussion of "naming" categories of evidence that support the hypothesis and turn it into a thesis. This discussion is found above in Chapter 7: Naming the Categories.

Sentence Structure

In the following section of this chapter, I present approximately 23 variations in sentence structure. Some will be very familiar to you; some will seem strange because they are from a high register of formality which you do not use. All are correct. If you practice these variations, your ability to enrich your term paper style will increase. Even in the advanced draft of your paper, I advise you to underline relevant parts of sentences and put in the margins the number of the variation according to my list. If, at first, you are not able to find 23 sentences that you can vary, I sincerely urge you to try harder before submitting your paper. There are other variations that are possible, but these are the basic variations apparently referred to in the rubric.

_____.

Variations

Structure   ## Example

1. INVERTING SENTENCE PARTS:

    A. Ramon has lived in New Orleans **for all of his life.**

    B. For all of his life, Ramon has lived in New Orleans.

    Comment: Any change, such as the above, results in a change: here, the change is that Sentence "B" expresses the writer's wish to stress the time involved. However, we do achieve a desirable variation in the structure of the sentence, which is well worth noting. The comma after "life" tells us that this phrase was moved out of its "canonical" or natural order.

2. –ING INITIAL: **Opening the box**, Bill thought of Susan.

    Comment: Often, it is necessary in English to move the modifying phrase next to the word that it modifies. Consider the sentence below:

    Loading their shotguns, the lions looked at the hunters.

    According to this sentence, it is the lions who were loading their shotguns. The structure is corrected below. The reason we moved the "loading" phrase was to put it near the word it modifies--"hunters."

    Loading their shotguns, <u>the hunters</u> watched the lions.

3. PARALLEL: A. I want to swim, eat and sleep.

    Comment: If the sentence is short, we do not have to insert the Parallel Marker "to" before "eat," and "sleep."

    If the sentence is longer, it is necessary to insert the marker:

    B. I want <u>to</u> swim in the morning before breakfast, <u>to</u> eat early in the afternoon before my business meetings when I am usually tense, and <u>to</u> sleep peacefully all night.

    Rule of Thumb: Insert the Parallel Marker before parallel elements. You will prevent confusion.

4. "WHAT" AS A LINK: I can do <u>**what**</u> I like.

5. "WHICH" WITH PREPOSITION:

    A. The car <u>in which</u> I was riding ____ was blue

    B. The car ____ <u>which</u> I was riding <u>in</u> was blue.

Comment: The preposition can be placed either before or after "which": it cannot be put in both places.

    C. The professor **<u>with whom</u>** I studied was a very quiet person.

Comment: In contemporary English, **"whom"** with an **"m"** is necessary only when it follows a preposition.

    D. The professor **<u>who</u>** I studied **<u>with</u>** was very quiet.

6. "THAT" AS A LINK: The book **<u>that</u>** Bill read was long.

7. "THAT" AS A SUBJECT: Everyone liked the book **<u>that</u>** was short.

8. NOUN CLAUSE AS SUBJECT:

    A. **<u>That</u>** <u>John likes Mary</u> is obvious.

    B. <u>What I do</u> is none of your business.

Comment: In both "A" and "B," **THAT** and **WHAT** makes the clause that follows a subject. More precisely, "that" and "what" make a noun or "noun-clause" or "nominal" out of the clause that follows. Once it is a nominal or noun, it can be used as a subject.

9. NOUN CLAUSE AS OBJECT OF PREPOSITION:

    A. **<u>In spite of</u>** <u>what happened at the dance</u>, Joe and I are still friends.

    B. **<u>Because of who Ed knows</u>**, the whole class is in trouble.

    C. Jim cannot **<u>live on</u>** <u>what he makes as a musician.</u>

10. INFINITIVE AS SUBJECT:

    A. <u>To dance with a movie star</u> is my dream.

    B. <u>To drink too much wine</u> will make me silly.

    C. <u>To study all night</u> will lower my performance on the test.

11. INFINITIVE AS COMPLEMENT:

    A. She wanted **<u>to run</u>**.

    B. My son bought it **<u>to make me happy</u>**.

12. A COLON CAN COME BEFORE AN EXAMPLE OR EXPLANATION:

    A. Jude needs attention: he will do anything to get it.

  Comment: The first clause states a general truth. The second clause is concerned with a result of the first.

13. A COLON CAN COME BEFORE A LIST AND AFTER "FOLLOW":

    A. I need **a few things: soap, eggs, and bread.**

    B. The <u>following</u> students passed the test**: <u>Ed, Sue, and Ann.</u>**

14. A COLON CAN SEPARATE AN INFINITIVE FROM A STATEMENT:

    A. <u>To drive or to take a taxi</u>: <u>that is what we must decide</u>.

    B. <u>To eat a chocolate-pecan cake</u>: <u>that would remove anxiety</u>.

15. SUBJECT OF AN UNTENSED VERB IS IN THE OBJECTIVE C ASE:

    A. The teacher wanted **<u>me to know</u>** that I would probably fail.

  Comment: **"Now <u>I think</u> that I will probably fail."** The infinitive "to know" does not have tense. The verb "think" does have tense.

16. "FOR" BEFORE SUBJECT PLUS INFINITIVE:

    A. <u>For me to go out with you</u> would be wrong: you are married.

    B. It is difficult **<u>for John to dance</u>**.

17. "DO + SO" AS A PRO-VERB:

    A. I asked him to leave and he **<u>did so</u>**.

    B. I love to drive; **<u>so does</u>** my son.

18. "SUCH" AS A PRO-ADJECTIVE:

    A. Jane has a **<u>new red car</u>**. Ed would like to have **<u>such a car</u>**.

19. "SUCH AS" WITH EXAMPLE:

    A. Many soft drinks, <u>**such as**</u> **Dandy Cola**, are made without sugar.

20. PAST PARTICIPLE AS ADJECTIVE PLACED FIRST IN SENTENCE:

    A. <u>**Designed**</u> **by an architect,** the house won many prizes.

    B. <u>**Painted**</u> **by an anonymous artist,** the mural was considered an excellent work of art.

21. A PREPOSITIONAL PHRASE CAN BE PLACED FIRST, FOLLOWED BY A COMMA:

    A. <u>**Without**</u> **a compass,** he wandered aimlessly.

22. A SEMICOLON AND A COMMA CAN BE USED TO JOIN REDUCED SENTENCES:

    A. John likes movies about war.

    B. Janet likes movies about romance.

Sentence "B" is identical to Sentence "A" except for "war" and "romance". Such sentences are boring. We can reduce them in the manner of "C" or "D" or "E" in which semicolon replaces the final period at the end of Sentence "A", and the comma replaces the duplicated part of the Verb Phrase. It is a judgment call as to how many parts can be replaced. Usually, the basic structures are identical.

    C. John likes movies about war; Janet, romance.

or

    D. John likes movies about war; Janet, about romance.

or

    E. John likes movies about war; Janet, movies about romance,

<u>**THE ABOVE REDUCTION (C, D, AND E) IS
VERY POPULAR AND SHOULD BE MASTERED!**</u>

23. Square brackets ([.....]) are used by an editor who wishes to indicate that the comments are his or hers and are not part of the text.

    Example: "The aging man who hated [here the manuscript is illegible] went into a rare fit of anger."

24. Three asterisks [###] in the center of the page can be used to mark the end of one piece of writing in a larger paper that itself deals another topic. [I agree that this practice is only distantly related to sentence structure. On the other hand, it does signify that one

set of sentences has come to an end, and that another is about to begin. Regardless, it is a convenient tool to have in your kit.]

Chapter 21:
Background

The very first line of your paper will be the title followed by your name as the author. Next will be a paragraph of no more than 50 words about your life as a student: this is called informally your "Bio" or "Bio-Blurb" or, a little more formally, your biographical sketch. Do not write "Bio-Blurb" in your paper: formally you can call it "Note on the Author." The reason I mention "Bio-Blurb," "biographical sketch" and "Note on the Author" is so that you will consider the term paper the formal product of a long and sometimes tedious and informal process, one in which you used scaffolding to put all of the pieces in place.

The next item will be an abstract in which you summarize—also in no more than 50 words--your old idea, new idea and evidence. Once you have done this preliminary work, you will present the second section which will consist of the Introduction and the Background. You will type the word "Introduction" two spaces above the first paragraph. (Please note that the lines of this paragraph are one space apart. The words "Chapter 21: Background" are two spaces above the paragraph.)

We will discuss the introduction after we look at the important "Background," in which you will summarize the approach that is generally held and respected at present. For us, the background is always concerned with what we have called the "old" idea. The old idea is that football is a good and proper sport for elementary and high school students. Our "New" idea or hypothesis is that football is dangerous and for several other reasons should be banned in elementary and high school.

In the background section, however, we are not interested in rejection. Instead, we wish to summarize the current attitude of acceptance in one or two paragraphs. In general, the background might well make up one tenth (2/20) of the entire paper. It might include a mention of the history of football. One very effective way to do this is to find typical reports in newspapers published in 1850 or in 1900 or in 1920 or 1960. In the background, we are not concerned with stating our hypothesis but with the situation before our hypothesis was introduced.

We will not be concerned with anything except that which supports football in schools. We might summarize the positive attitude towards football among parents, students and coaches. We might describe briefly a football game at which there is a crowd, a band, cheerleaders, lights, and lots of excitement. It is the ambience of the football game and the positive attitude towards the sport that are important in the background. In subsequent parts of this paper, we will attempt to provide evidence that football is bad for students: To provide contrast—here "good" and "bad"—is usually one mark of clear, effective writing.

I present below an acceptable "Background" for our Practice Term Paper which was written by a student in the first of two courses in English Composition. The total length of this representative term paper is 1,000 original—not quoted--words. The length of the "Background" section is—according to an earlier chapter--2/20 of the total words (2/20 x 1,000 = 100 words). The subhead will be "Background." In the sample below, there are 102 words, not counting the quotation. The author cites one source to bolster the "old idea" contention that football is one means of a young man demonstrating to his community that he is becoming fully a man. It is important that note be taken that the words in a quotation are not to be used in the total count of 1,000. The name of the author was not given but the article appeared on a site named "Direct Essays." I retrieved this article on 13 September 2012. Immediately following is the citation format:

"Boys to Men: How Boys Develop Masculinity Through Sports." *Direct Essays.* Retrieved on 13 September 2012. www.directessays.com/viewpaper/39738.html.

****

Background

It is believed by a great many people that sports offer teenagers a chance to demonstrate that they are making a successful transition to maturity by the self-discipline and cooperation necessary in the activity itself. One anonymous eighteen-year-old put it succinctly: "I believe that developing masculinity through sports is important in building character for a young boy who transitions into manhood....I believe masculinity is an essential component for a man who enters adulthood and becomes a father and a husband." This author goes on to say that it is sometimes necessary to suffer physical injury in the game of baseball in order for a player's team to win. This equation of masculinity with self-discipline and suffering injury for the sake of the team is part of the Rite of Passage without which a boy rarely becomes a responsible adult.

****

Chapter 22:

The "Introduction" to the Term Paper

The first major part of an academic paper is often entitled "Introduction." This word appears two spaces above the text and under the required title, the name of the person who wrote the paper, his or her "Bio" and the abstract (see Chapter 18). The title is a necessary part of any formal piece of writing. It is the main "head" and will be followed by "subheads" such as "Introduction," "Background" and "Conclusion." I prefer that the entire paper be in Times New Roman. The title will be in 14-point font, and the name of the student author will be in 12-point font. I also prefer that all titles and subheads be centered and that they be in boldface.

****

Figure 11. Example of Fonts for Title and Author. The main title should be in 14 point type. The name of the author should be in 12 point. Both should be in boldface.

Football:
A Sport Whose Time Has Come and Gone
by
Kevin Gonzalez

****

The reason we have not yet discussed the introduction is that it is probably the most important part to get right. I wanted you to get the feel of what we were doing before going into it in detail. According to the model I am presenting, there are several major parts to the introduction:

1. **Opening information**
2. **Brief Statement of "Old" Idea**
3. **Thesis Statement (or "New" Idea)**
4. **Naming of Categories of Evidence**

As we have said, the thesis statement is the single most important sentence or sentences in the paper. It must be very clear and definite. The thesis statement should normally be confined to at most 30 words and not extend to a second sentence unless absolutely necessary. The very first sentence should attract the reader to the paper: that is the main purpose of the opening information. An example follows:

First Sentence with "Opening Information"

Football is often thought to be an excellent place for a youngster to demonstrate that he is becoming a man.

Brief Statement of "Old" Idea

The exposure, the physicality, the padded uniform and helmet, the team-work required--all of these would seem to make this the ideal sport for a young man to prove his worth as a member of the adult world.

Transition from Old to New

Yet there is a darker, more troubling side that is so serious that it is bringing many persons to a fairly extreme position.

Thesis Statement

Opponents of football say that this sport should be banned from elementary and high school, primarily because of the physical, mental, and moral damage it can cause.

Naming of Categories of Evidence

We will explore these reasons in terms of (1) serious injuries, (2) the lesson that violence can lead to winning, (3) the embarrassment of the players who dress out but do not get to play, and (4) the number of students who do not participate in any way in this expensive sport.

NOTA BENE: To avoid confusion, I will present the several parts of my introduction exactly as they would appear in the term paper. They are the same as printed above.

****

Introduction

Football is often thought to be an excellent place for a youngster to demonstrate that he is becoming a man. The exposure, the physicality, the padded uniform and helmet, the team-work required--all of these would seem to make this the ideal sport for a young man to prove his worth as a member of the adult world. Yet there is a darker, more troubling side that is so serious that it is bringing many persons to a fairly extreme position. Opponents of football say that this sport should be banned from elementary and high school, primarily because of the physical, mental, and moral damage it can cause. We will explore these reasons in terms of (1) serious injuries, (2 the lesson that violence can lead to winning, (3) the embarrassment of the players who dress out but do not get to play, and (4) the number of students who do not participate in any way in this expensive sport.

****

Chapter 23:
Illustrations, Tables and Figures

The careful arrangements of words can be helpful to us in ordering our thoughts and bringing them to a realization that we can expect our readers to share. But there comes a point at which those words get in the way. It is at this point that "a picture is worth a thousand words," as the popular saying goes. Such cases certainly can arise in the course of writing a term paper. Although it is never acceptable to use illustrations, tables and figures as mere decoration, they are quite welcome if they will help in the articulation and clarification of an idea or theory. There is often a point at which our progress across the wide river of words needs something in addition to subheads, size of font, and typeface to get across. If there is doubt as to whether or not an illustration, table or figure is justified, then it is in order to think of these as a necessary life-raft.

If you see in some publication an interesting photo that illustrates very well what you are writing about, there is a probability that the publication will grant you permission to copy and use it. A lawyer can specialize in copyright law and bring sophisticated arguments to support his or her client. I say this to illustrate the complexity of the right to copy an intellectual property. Usually, issues arise only if a large sum of money is involved or if one person does not want his contribution to become anonymous. Therefore, if we give full credit to the person and/or the magazine in which we found the copyrighted material, we will have avoided impropriety. A reader might also be interested in consulting the original source so that he can make certain that the writer of the term paper did not misrepresent the issue. If your instructor sees that you are conscientious and careful in the matter of copyrights, that instructor will tend to respect you as a responsible student and writer.

It is of considerable importance that you do not use the illustration, table or figure as a decoration. Instead, use it only in close relationship to a point you are making in the text. You should group all illustrations together in numerical order; all tables in numerical order; and all figures in numerical order. Briefly, an illustration is a picture-like representation of information. A figure includes any graph-like representation. A table usually is centered around columns of numbers. You should place them after the list of chapters in the table of contents as was done in this book. You should number and name the item, and write enough words to explain what it is doing. You might well consult Figures 1-13 on this volume for examples.

###

Chapter 24:
Models for Cover Sheet, Research Report

When I was 21 years old, I went to work as a reporter for moderate-size daily newspaper. I had not studied journalism and did not know the first thing about graphic design. Vince, my editor was a cordial man of few words. Few days passed, however, during the first three months when he did not tell me at least one thing about how to catch the reader's eye without enormous headlines and splashy photographs.. One of the trade secrets I learned was to use a lot of subheads in the story. Another was to vary the size of the headlines. The end result of all these lessons was some ability to use a variety of means to avoid masses of uniform print facing the reader. Such is bad design: it makes readers feel that they are diving into a deep sea and have no choice but to keep swimming until they have reached the other side. They should, my editor said, find little islands of photos and subheads where they could rest for a moment. Simplistic, you might say, but take a look at any page in any professional textbook and you will see that the graphic designer has worked his or her magic. That is one reason for subheads.

The other is that when readers read a subhead, they will expect to see related items of information under it. This is very simple but very good advice when you are trying to organize your term paper in such a way that it be rated high on the rubric. Going from Old Idea to New Idea and then Listing the Categories in one enumerated sentence is the way we will begin. Vary from this and you will be inviting trouble. The next section will be the Background followed by the detailed presentation of Categories of Evidence that are arranged in the same order as you listed them in the first section. The Conclusion will be the shortest section of your paper. The last section--called "Works Cited"--will be the list of all of the sources from which you collected the bits and pieces of information that you assembled. Conscientious writers also list sources that they did not use and name, but that they think readers might be interested in. Such a more comprehensive list is called a "Bibliography."

At this juncture, we will turn to the articulation of the title, the Main Head from which the Subheads are taken. You can use a maximum of nine words in the title, and those words cannot form a question or a sentence. The following title is terrible because it is a complete sentence: "*The Social Order in Prison Reflects Power not Democracy." (The asterisk [*] denotes that something is wrong with the word or sentence that follows it.) It is a convention of academic writing that the title will not be a question or a sentence. We can change this to "The Source of Order in Prison: Power not Democracy." The colon (":") has replaced the verb "is." Now the title passes muster: it is acceptable. It is appalling and naive to believe that you can change a convention at will. To try is the mark of the rank amateur.

In Figure 10, there is a model for a cover sheet and a research report. In the latter report, please note that some of the items required for information from sources Printed on Paper is different from that of information derived from the internet, sometimes called "Printed on Screen." In some cases, it is virtually impossible to identify the name of the source, i.e., the publisher or person who has posted a given article. In such cases, you are not to use the information in your paper.

I have placed the following publications on reserve in the University Library: *Term Papers and Preformed Language: Keys to Academic Writing* and *Student's Guide to Writing College Papers* (MLA and APA) by Kate L. Turabian. You are welcome to use this material. Although I prefer the style of the Modern Language Association (MLA), you may use that of the American Psychological Association (APA) or that of *The Chicago Manual of Style* if you prefer. On page 301 of the third edition of the *MLA Style Manual and Guide to Scholarly Publishing* (2008), you will find a total of fifteen style manuals, each of which differs from the others in the details of documentation. If you should find yourself interested, I would be glad to point you to a librarian on campus who is competent in such relatively esoteric matters.

****

Figure 12: Forms for Copying-- Cover Sheet, Research Report. Form 'A' is a model for your cover sheet. It will come before any other material.

A.

Football:
A Sport Whose Time Has Come and Gone
by
Kevin Gonzalez

A Term Paper Prepared
for
Dr. Clyde Coreil

Submitted in the Completion
of Part of the Requirements

of

English Composition 1
at
New Jersey City University

on

April 16, 2012

****

B. Form for Submission of Research Report: Please attach the sheet on the following page to printouts, duplicated pages or similar source. Note: "(O)" is primarily for online sources.

Research Report Number _____

_____   _____
Name of Student   Date Submitted

1. Author(s): (last name first) (O): _____

2. Date of Publication (O): _____

3. Main Title (in italics) (O): _____

4. Edition Number: _____

5. Name(s) of Editors: _____

6. Place of Publication: _____

7. Publisher: _____

8. Agency of Publication (O): _____

9. Date of Retrieval (O): _____

10. Complete Electronic Address (O): Note: If this is the same as in Item 11, write "See below." _____

_____

_____

_____

11. Bibliographic Format (O): Please repeat the above information, arranging it as you would in a citation listed in the "Bibliography" or "Works Cited" or "References."

_____

_____

_____

_____

_____

_____

_____

12. Example of Bibliographic Format (O):

Smithson, David (1974). "Cats and Speech" in *Non-Human Communication*, Helen
    F. Gates, ed. Louisiana State University Press: Baton Rouge. Retrieved on 04 April 2012.
    <http//www.cats.speech.LSU.BR/1.2.3.zin7.univerpress//louisiana/main.camp>

13. Other Information (O): _____

_____

_____

_____

_____

_____

_____

_____

****

Chapter 25:
Documentation

A "citation" is a short, stylized note stating exactly where you found the words or specific ideas that support your thesis statement. In the text, in the immediate vicinity of the specific information in question, you should place--within parentheses--the last name of the author and the number of the page on which you found the information. For example: (Coreil, 55). The preceding constitutes a parenthetical or "running" note. Expanded versions of these notes are entered in alphabetical order as the very last element in any publication. It is important to use "reverse indentation"--sometimes called "hanging indentation"-- when listing these (See Figure 13). If the citation refers to a particular set of pages or to a chapter in a given book by one set of authors, the number of the relevant pages follows the name of the publisher and the place of publication.

It seems that editors have gone too far in their effort to save printed letters and to reduce the number of capital letters. I find this reduction awkward and confusing. Last names followed by initials are fine unless you need to use a personal pronoun (he or she, his or her) in the text. One does not know if "Herbert, R.L." is a man or a woman. And one can never assume that the writer is the Richard Lee Herbert one met at a convention last year. So in the papers you write for me, you will use the name exactly as it appears under the title of the source you consulted.

If you are naming an article that appeared in a larger anthology, give that name exactly as you saw it in your source. The words--India: the country of a thousand dialects--will revert to "India: The Country of a Thousand Dialects." Sometimes the entire main title of the publication will be rendered: *Second and foreign language learning through classroom interaction.* If an article from that anthology is mentioned in that citation, the only difference will be that the article will be in regular font and the title will be in italics. In short, for me, the important nouns are capitalized and quotation marks enclose articles. The main title is not enclosed in quotation marks; important words are capitalized, and the font is italics.

****

Figure 13. Example of Bibliographic Entry: Following in "A" is a typical bibliographic entry for an article by Louis Davis entitled "Variations in the Lower Elementary Curriculum" in an anthology entitled *International Education* that was published in 2011 by Valino Publications, which is located in Santa Fe, New Mexico [USA]. This entry credits Davis and provides enough information for an interested reader to acquire a copy of the publication

———————————

A.

Davis, Louis (2011). "Variations in the Lower Elementary Curriculum" in *International Education.* Santa Fe, New Mexico: Valino Publications.

———————————

In "B" is a typical citation for information from the internet. The author is Grady Kartel. The article being cited appeared on pages 11-18 in Print on Paper on February 10, 2012 and was announced or "posted" on the internet on February 21, 2012 in a magazine entitled *Adventures Abroad*. The information was retrieved by the researcher on June 21, 2012. The relevant URL address is <http://www.bsa.study>.

B.
Kartel, Grady. *Adventures Abroad,* 10 Feb. 2012: 11-18. Posted,
    21 February 2012. Retrieved on 21 June 2012. <http://www. bsa.study>.

****

There are two main methods of such documentation: the Modern Language Association (MLA) method and the American Psychological Association (APA) method. Either is acceptable. Because I prefer the MLA style of citing sources, that is the one I will discuss here. It should be noted that there is a good deal of basic similarity among the great many styles of documentation used in publications within the United States of America and abroad. In general, the editors apparently survey their needs as far as what ancillary information they wish to include as non-text material. They then design their documentation to be a sensible combination of (1) their needs and (2) accepted styles such as those found in MLA and APA guides. Foremost in their minds seems to be a wish to make it clear to their readers what they are doing. They have succeeded marvelously.

Deciding What Needs to be Documented

Early on, we must decide whether or not the specific piece of information given in the term paper needs to be mentioned. For example, if I say, "There are many large cities in the world," this is considered common knowledge and does not need citation. If, on the other hand, I say that women are significantly happier in large cities than men, I need to give the source because the reader can be expected to ask how do I know that. If the increase in happiness is something I just seem to feel but have not seen in print or heard anywhere, under no conditions can I mention this dubious increase in the term paper. If I were writing a personal essay, then I might consider including such a statement. In academic writing, however, I am forced to rely on objective evidence.

I can use the opinion of others as given in a survey. If this survey was printed and if I expect readers to be interested, I should insert that survey itself in what is called the "Appendix" between the body of the paper and the bibliography, which is always the last and final section in a term paper. Of course, I will write a letter to the publisher explaining that I am requesting permission to reprint the survey in the term paper I am writing. If you do write such a letter and get a positive response, you should state after the full name and date of the survey, that permission to use the survey in your term paper was granted by the publisher.

If I did indeed see in a reputable source a mention of this increase in the happiness of women, I give information on it in two places--one short and one long. The short, abbreviated citation will be given immediately after the sentence and before the period: (Higgins, 156). The longer, complete citation will be given in the bibliography, which is a list of sources that I used in the term paper. A list that is called "Works Cited" is limited to the sources I actually referred to in the text .("References" is another term for Works Cited.) The subhead "Bibliography" indicates that the list includes sources not mentioned in the term paper but that the writer thinks the reader might like to know about.

For sources found on the internet, it is necessary to put--at the end of the citation--the date you retrieved (found) the information on the internet immediately before you give the complete electronic address enclosed by angled brackets. For example:

Retrieved on 23 Jan 2010 <http:www.gde/edu/web/dtereot/698>

The main reason I ask that you give the complete electronic address at the end of the entry is simply because often it is very long and might confuse the reader. One rule of thumb is this: once you have settled on a system for documentation, use that system and only that system. Be consistent. Readers expect it and will be irritated if consistency is not present.

The term "Annotation" is used for a note to the reader written in complete sentences and containing relevant information that cannot be summarized in a bibliographic citation. Sections of annotations are sometimes placed at the bottom of the pages of the text or at the end before the bibliography. The year of publication of any book can be found on the Publication Information Page, which is on the rear of the official title page. You should always consult these two pages for complete titles, publishers' names, and dates of copyright and/or publication.

The best-known "bible" of documentation and academic writing in general was compiled by Kate L. Turabian and edited in several versions, such as *Student's Guide to Writing College Papers* (2010). She explains an enormous number of possible variations in citing references. A much shorter book is the *Modern Languages Association Handbook*, which offers easy explanations of how to document a term paper.

One way in I differ with the *MLA Handbook* is in my requiring only single spacing between citation entries in the bibliography. Space is a very valuable commodity in any printed-on-paper or printed-on-screen presentation. There is—in my opinion--no good reason for double-spacing in the bibliography. In addition, I personally find that double-spacing between lines of the text of the term paper is annoying. I accept double-spacing, but I prefer single spacing. Single-spacing increases considerably the coherence in the appearance of the material, especially in extended quotations of six lines or more. In Figure 14, I attempt to indicate one acceptable way of arranging text with reference to indentation.

****

Figure 14. Guide to Spacing and Indentation

A. Indent all paragraphs by approximately one inch.

B. Use standard borders of one inch from top, bottom and right hand side. For the left-hand side, use a border of one and a half inches.

C. For extended quotations of five or more lines, indent one and a half inches.

D. The space before and after extended quotations and Figures should be approximately double the space between lines of text.

E. I prefer one space between lines of text. However, the use of two spaces between lines of the text is acceptable.

****

Another way in which I differ with past issues of the *MLA Handbook* is in the use of underlines to indicate the major titles in a citation. More recent editions suggest hitting the computer key to change from "regular" font to "italic" font. This is what I expect you to do.

Although it is good to remember the order in which elements are presented in the citation, it is also wise and good to have on hand a reputable article with a bibliography to consult. Use it as a model. There is nothing wrong with that. The end result will be a term paper that bears the standard features of professionally executed writing. Such a bibliography is also on library reserve. Please use the model in Chapter 24 for the cover sheet of your term paper. It is somewhat formal, but it is correct and will probably help you feel good about the work you have put into your term paper.

Kinds of Documentation

Some 43,500 journals cover specific areas of all fields studied in the university, trades, businesses and industries. Usually, however, the term "journal" is reserved for a rather formal publication that comes out approximately once every three months or once a year. The word carries with it the aura of higher education. So much is this the case that the term "juried publication" or "refereed journal" is often mentioned in academic requirements regarding advancement and promotion.

The "jury" is usually a group of between five and twelve experts from different universities in the academic area covered by the specific journal. In addition to the editor, one or two of these experts must read and approve the articles published by a journal: the experts judge the quality of thesis, evidence and writing. If they do not approve, the article is rejected by the particular journal. Once that happens, the writer is free to revise and resubmit the article, or to send it to another publication.

If a college professor does not have at least several articles in juried publications, he or she is often denied renewal of contract, or--after five or six renewals--the prized status of tenure. Once a person has tenure, it is difficult for the institution of higher learning to terminate the individual. Usually, being published in an academic journal takes a great deal of time. Accordingly, many professors spend a great many hours researching and writing articles which they constantly send out. One well known phrase regarding this is, "Publish or perish."

The other path to tenure involves outstanding service to the university or to a given field of study. Service and/or publications are of great importance in the employment of university teachers. This requirement is often overlooked, and the university professor is criticized because he or she has only twelve or fifteen hours of classroom contact each week. Elementary and secondary teachers usually do not have to meet service and publications requirements.

Publication is probably the most important expectation of university faculty members. The reason I mention it here is that many of you will work in education after you get an undergraduate degree from this university. I strongly advise those of you who are in this category to pay close attention to recent publications in the field you expect to enter. If you are wise, you will take this course and this textbook very seriously. It could mean the difference between recognized success in your field, and being unrecognized. The ability, willingness and readiness to write at a professional paper is definitely a distinguishing factor in any profession.

It is not likely that persons interested in automobile repair would name their publication "The Journal of Transmission Repair" although that is a very sophisticated trade that might very well have a publication and many readers. This is relevant to the writing of term papers because relevant evidence will come from wherever we find it: in a journal, trade publication, military manual, radio or television broadcast, newspaper, news letter, commercial publication, instruction booklet on refrigerator repair or any other relevant and reliable source. Although the writer is expected to consult any of these, he is not expected or allowed to use the informal style of writing found in them.

The internet is an enormous source of information, but the persons who write and edit these sources is often untrustworthy. To assure that the information we cite is reliable, many journals have an editorial board or jury made up of well known professionals. The very well known online reference publication *Wikipedia* has a very low standing in sophisticated circles because virtually anyone can add or change any item of information at will without the approval of an editor or board. Because of this serious difficulty, we will not cite as evidence information from *Wikipedia* in our term papers. To do so would probably mark one as an unsophisticated, untrustworthy amateur. For your information, if you cite *Wikipedia* in serious conversation, you will be considered poorly educated. Forewarned is forearmed.

###

Chapter 26:
Writing in the Right Voice: Formal vs. Informal

There is a great divide between Narrative Writing and Academic Writing. Neither is good or bad in itself. To put it as simply as possible, narrative is used in telling stories; academic writing is involved in proposing a hypothesis and developing objective evidence to support it. If I use narrative in academic writing, it is always bad. If I use the academic style to tell a story, that is bad--or even worse, it is terrible.

In most beginning classes, the teacher wants to help students become able to use subjects, verbs and objects in making a sentence. This is most easily done by teaching students to write essays of opinion, accounts of what they did during their vacation, and possibly even short stories. The students were welcome to use the first person "I" and "we," the second person "you," and the third person "he, she, it, her, they, them." If it fit the narrative, they were welcome to use these pronouns. In academic writing, we stay away from narrative and we do not use personal pronouns. Why not? Because convention does not allow it. If you do not follow convention, you will be considered poorly educated. Period.

Another feature of the narrative is the use of emotions such as love, hate, admiration, fear, bravery, cowardice, intimidation, praise, and fascination. It is not only possible but praiseworthy if students keep those emotions in mind as they are developing the piece of writing. To engage in academic writing, however, is a different ball game. Personal pronouns are not used, and emotion is to be avoided like the plague, a serious disease. Replacing emotion is the absolutely unemotional statement of hypothesis, and the objective presentation of evidence to make a compelling case. It is wonderful to be passionate about writing term papers: it is like jumping off a cliff to say anything that will betray your emotion. Do it and suffer. Forewarned is forearmed.

One effective means of breaking the habit of using narrative is to "break" the term paper into sections like those in the "Skeletal Outline of Academic Paper" in Chapter 17: Organization: Broad Principles. We said that the preliminary parts are, in order: (A) Title, (B) Author, (C) Bio-Blurb, and (D) Abstract. At this point, we will not look further into sections A-D. We will limit ourselves to the nine sections presented below:

Skeletal Outline of Academic Paper

	1. Old Idea
INTRODUCTION————	**2. New Idea**
	3. Naming of Categories of Evidence
BACKGROUND————	**4. Background**
	5. Discussion of 1st Category of Evidence
EVIDENCE————————	**6. Discussion of 2nd Category of Evidence**
	7. Discussion of 3rd Category of Evidence

8. Discussion of 4th Category of Evidence

CONCLUSION———— 9. Conclusion

Ongoing Accounts

It is a main goal of this chapter to make you aware that in all writing there is "voice" and "point of view." It is absolutely necessary that we learn to recognize and use different elements of voice in writing that is casual as well as writing that is formal. I recall that once President John Kennedy was addressed as "Mr. President" by his younger brother, Robert. John Kennedy smiled and said that that level of formality was not necessary. Robert astutely pointed out that in his opinion, it was. John Kennedy was the President and had some enormous responsibilities. The younger brother was aware that in his older brother, there was also the man who was serving in the highest office in the country. When they were relaxing in the White House, they were brothers. When John Kennedy was making an important decision in the Oval Office, he was indeed the President.

We must become aware of the differences in the voice with which we talk about fishing and football, and the voice we use in writing formal term papers. The writing we will do in this chapter will be informal. We will talk informally about what we did to find the things we will use in writing the very formal term paper. We will learn to control these and not use the formal voice in an informal situation. And vice versa.

The Ongoing Accounts with which we are concerned in this chapter is very different from the Research Reports we discussed in Chapter 24. That was concerned primarily with one of the specific pieces of evidence you collected and will likely present in the Final Term Paper. In this chapter, you will be talking and writing Ongoing Accounts of the work you are doing each week, work that will be like the scaffolding placed around a building while it is under construction. When you are finished writing the Final Term Paper, these Ongoing Accounts will disappear.

You should photocopy the following page and use it as a cover sheet for occasional informal reports you make to your instructor. For each assignment, you will write an informal 300-word description of your work on, for example, Section 1. The Old Idea. You might start out by discussing the manner in which you chose one of the 70 questions in Chapter 19. Then you will write about the contemporary attitudes that surround what you will call the "Old Idea." You will mention anything you did to help develop your topic. You will be required to go beyond the computer to conduct an interview with at least one person who has had real-world experience in your topic. You will also write letters or send e-mail to such persons. You will be responsible for going beyond your comfortable computer and breathing life into this project. If you remain at your comfortable computer, your grade will suffer.

For example, if your topic concerns women and prison, you might write to or interview someone in law enforcement who is able to provide information that is relevant to your term paper. Your instructor will be able to tell if you were committed to your project in terms of time and effort. One of the main reasons for these Ongoing Accounts is to make sure that you are focusing your efforts on these assignments. They are closely tied to your performance in researching and writing the final term paper, which, in turn, is very important to your performance in this class. This paper can, in fact, constitute a capstone achievement in your study of English. If you take yourself, your studies and indeed your career seriously, you will write a paper of which both you and your instructor can be proud.

Cover Sheet
Ongoing Account of Section(s) #_____

Practice in Completing
The Different Parts of the Term Paper

Instructor: _____ Student: _____

Date: _____ Name of University: _____

Which of the 70 questions in Chapter 19 are you using to develop a topic?

I am working with question number _____ which I copy on the next lines:

_____

_____

In 300 words, discuss your progress as assigned. Attach (staple) your writing to this cover sheet. Occasionally, your instructor will ask you to make a comment in the space below.

Chapter 27: Evidence—
In Text, Appendix, or Bibliography?

A decision must be made on where to place evidence that supports the thesis--in the text itself, in the Appendix, or in the Bibliography often called "Works Cited." The basis for that decision is relevance and importance. When I was discussing lexical structure and categorization, the strongest and only examples I could think of was Dexter Jeffries and Black Bear. Jeffries questioned the legitimacy of considering "race" as a real category. Black Bear had difficulty with the lexical structure of the word "Art," which, for him, did not name a substantial category. The evidence was crucial to my argument, so I placed it in the text itself.

The text of the entire article that supported my use of the concept of preformulation was of great importance to what I had to say about that structure, so I included it in the Appendix of the present book. The names of the publications that essentially used different words for "preformulations" were certainly relevant but not of the importance of "race" and "art." I put them in the Bibliography. To leave out the names of those publications would not have been, in my opinion, responsible.

The arena in which I was participating was academia, which has no membership list for universities or for individual persons. When a person asks to be heard by others in academia, he is saying that his or her honor, reputation and status itself are behind his request and that he or she will not say or do anything that is not carefully in keeping with the standards of that community. That includes the careful representation of the words or deeds of another. The decision of how to most responsibly set forth evidence is part of that code of conduct. Ultimately, the decision is yours to make--not only as a student in this class, but as a junior member of academia. Do not take this lightly.

Appendix: A Useful Pocket for Items of Importance

The word "appendant" is not used often but indicates a relationship in which one thing is not intimately a part of a main body. The word "appendix" refers either to a part of a book or to the end of the intestine. Both meanings are closely associated with appendant. The appendix can be thought of as a useful pocket in which are kept things that are not an integral part of the text but that we want to be printed with it and not to be allowed to stray. An "insert" is the word used to refer to something that the publisher wants to place between the pages but which is much farther away than the matter at hand. The appendix of a book can contain photographs, prayers, transcribed interviews, quotations from another source that are mentioned in the text, copies of military orders, letters, copies of postage stamps, poems, written songs, diplomas, and things of that sort. I personally am drawn to appendices which I sometimes find to be more interesting then the text.

The location of the appendix is always after the body of the text and before the bibliography. It is entitled "Appendix" and is never combined with any other section. It is not considered part of the bibliography and is virtually never left out of subsequent printings. In the next chapter of the present text, I have included a sample term paper, and have placed in the Appendix part of the transcribed interview. I would not place in the Appendix the printout of a website or other sources that could be located by a reader. Rather, I would include that information in the bibliography or "Works Cited" section.

If you have more than one item--for example, a photograph and an interview--You should enumerate each and write two or three sentences describing each item. For example, if you are presenting two photographs, you should describe each, saying (1) What is described in each photograph, (2) Who took the photo, (3) On what date was the photo taken, (4) Where was it published or how did you acquire it, and any other information that might be relevant. Then, under each photo, you should summarize the above information in from 3 to 15 words in boldfaced font. In other words, you will present up to 50 words of description before the item and, if possible, from 3-15 words following the item.

This presentation of items in the Appendix will be optional in the Practice Term Paper completed in the first half of the course. It will be required in the Real Term Paper completed in the second half of the course. One acceptable means of presenting this material is illustrated below:

****

Appendix

Following is a mockup of a photograph that might appear in the appendix to a term paper related to civil unrest in the period from 1950-1970 in the USA. The photograph was taken by the fictional Dwight B. Highson and published in the Newark Advertiser Gazette on January 1, 1968. Permission for its use in this term paper was obtained by the author.

```
XXXXXXXXXXXXXXXXXXXXXXXXXXXXXXXXXX
XXXXXXXXXXXXXXXXXXXXXXXXXXXXXXXXXX
XXXXXXXXXXXXXXXXXXXXXXXXXXXXXXXXXX
XXXXXXXXXXXXXXXXXXXXXXXXXXXXXXXXXX
XXXXXXXXXXXXXXXXXXXXXXXXXXXXXXXXXX
XXXXXXXXXXXXXXXXXXXXXXXXXXXXXXXXXX
XXXXXXXXXXXXXXXXXXXXXXXXXXXXXXXXXX
XXXXXXXXXXXXXXXXXXXXXXXXXXXXXXXXXX
XXXXXXXXXXXXXXXXXXXXXXXXXXXXXXXXXX
XXXXXXXXXXXXXXXXXXXXXXXXXXXXXXXXXX
XXXXXXXXXXXXXXXXXXXXXXXXXXXXXXXXXX
XXXXXXXXXXXXXXXXXXXXXXXXXXXXXXXXXX
XXXXXXXXXXXXXXXXXXXXXXXXXXXXXXXXXX
XXXXXXXXXXXXXXXXXXXXXXXXXXXXXXXXXX
```

Unrest in Newark, New Jersey. Anthony Dreson (left) and Theo Smith, both of Newark, defend themselves against rock-throwing teenagers in the early hours of the riot. (Copyright photo. Dwight B. Highson, 1968)

Chapter 28:
A Sample Term Paper

The following piece of writing is in the format of a regular term paper, yet it is shorter because it was in reality a Practice Term Paper: often in brevity there is comprehension. It was written in preparation for a longer paper to be done independently in the second half of the course. For the practice paper, I assigned the entire class the same topic—the banning of football in elementary and secondary school. I did this so that we could all see similarities in structure, handling of evidence, documentation, and general format.

My contribution to the paper presented below was a sharply limited amount of editing here and there--far less than I sometimes did for articles I published as editor of *The Journal of the Imagination in Language Learning* (Coreil). I also suggested a first part of the introduction to make certain that students would work within the parameters of the persuasive or argumentative "old idea/new idea." The student used the model cover sheet provided in Chapter 24, and stayed away from the decorative flowers and other designs on the cover and in the interior of the paper itself. If a chart, photograph or illustration is directly relevant to the matter being discussed in the paper, it is welcome. Otherwise, it is unprofessional, naive and most unwelcome. Variation, interest and even elegance should come out of the argument itself--not out of the presence of colors and amusing drawings on the pages. In any form of academic writing, those are strictly prohibited.

The results of this "practice paper" were generally satisfactory. This is the first time I tried such an assignment, and I do indeed look forward to the independent projects. The student was in the first of two courses in composition. In our Program in English as a Second Language, students study for one 14-week semester in English Composition I: ESL, and for a comparable second semester in English Composition II; ESL. Because these courses satisfy all English requirements, they are taught for six credit hours each.

[It is with sadness that I report that yesterday on television, I saw Erik Waters, a college football player, fall during a game. He simply hit the back of his head against the ground: no one else was immediately involved. He was wearing a helmet that did not come off. Once he had fallen, he did not move. A stretcher cart was rolled to him, and he was gently lifted onto the vehicle and taken from the field--never having moved in the least. This appears to have been a very serious injury that could affect the entire future of Mr. Waters. The relevance of this statement is that the Practice Term Paper below was concerned with the banning of football as a school sport because of the possibility of physical injury.]

For the sake of clarity, the Practice Term Paper begins on the following page.

Football: No Longer A Rite of Passage

by

Adrienne Camille Lopez

A Practice Term Paper Prepared

for

Professor Clyde Coreil

**Submitted in the Completion
of Part of the Requirements**

of

English Composition I: ESL

at

New Jersey City University

on

October 25, 2012

Football: No Longer a Rite of Passage
by
Adrienne Camille Lopez

Note on the Author

Adrienne Camille Lopez is a junior at New Jersey City University in Jersey City, NJ. Although she has studied Nursing for three years, she has decided to leave the medical field and pursue Early Childhood and Special Education. More precisely, she is interested in working with younger children who have disabilities.

Abstract

Football has been often perceived as a sport that will allow a young man to prove that he is ready to take on the responsibility of manhood. However, football is no longer a rite of passage due to several factors that fail to support this common assumption.

Introduction

Football is often thought to be an excellent place for a youngster to demonstrate that he is becoming a man. The exposure, the physicality, the padded uniform and helmet, the team-work required—all of these would seem to add to the mystery and to make this the ideal sport for a young man to prove his worth as a member of the adult world. No other activity weds grace and agility to brawn and physical power in such a dramatic manner. Both are necessary in the real world, and it appears that football is a near-perfect blend of moment-to-moment reality and articulate metaphor.

Yet there is a darker, more troubling aspect--so serious that it is bringing many persons to a fairly extreme position. Opponents of football say that this sport should be banned from elementary and high school, primarily because of the physical, mental, and moral damage it can cause. We will explore these reasons in terms of (1) injuries to the head and brain, (2) the learning of the unacceptable lesson that sheer violence can lead to acceptable success, (3) the embarrassment of the players when they lose the game, and (4) the expense that the school and the players put into the sport of football.

Background

The great advantage of football is that it is a relatively controlled channel for a young man who is becoming a man. It has been often treated as the greatest of sports one can engage in. To be good at football is what almost every young man aspires to achieve. The sport is of considerable value in dramatizing and teaching the meaning of aspiration itself. As one author has put it, "Sport is important because it allows males to prove their masculinity" (West, 2010). This is repeated in an anonymous essay published online by *Direct Essays*. With the Friday-night game as a center, an entire ritual of bands, funny hats, cheering squads, cheer leaders and meaningful victory has emerged. For many students in a wide variety of ways, participation in an activity related to football has become a veritable and valuable Rite of Passage.

Injuries

Countering this tradition is the seriousness of the injury that football can cause to the head and brain of the young athletes. This sport has enabled families to gather together to support and root for the respective teams that they want to win. However, we often only see what is going on in the field but never really look into what is happening off the field. Though football can be a really entertaining game, deleterious brain injuries have increased among high school football players. As one article has stated, "Despite a widespread educational effort and rule changes designed to make the game safer, 13 high school football players suffered catastrophic brain injuries nationally in 2011" (Stevens, 2012). Football should be reevaluated by schools in regards to whether or not they will continue to allow students to engage in such sport because of the harmful effects that it could bring.

Violence

Not only is football violent, but it can be the cause of violence off the field. People who are huge fans of football tend to be very into the game. In an intense match, we would often see that both players and fans of respective teams gets rowdy and boo the team who becomes the lead if they are not for the team who is winning. An example that has transpired states that, "A football game between Berkeley High School and Oakland Tech was canceled Thursday because of fears that a violent confrontation could break out between adult spectators from two East Bay neighborhoods" (Zamora, 2003). Tension could rise in both players and non-players which may cause physical or emotional violence if the teasing be taken seriously. And interestingly enough, the article also states that "the rumored fights and feuding had nothing to do with players" (Zamora, 2003.) The rough-and-tumble ambience can easily get out of hand. We see that even mere spectators who are not included in the game itself can bring possible arguments that lead to confrontation and fighting.

Embarrassment

Football players feel a sense of embarrassment when they lose a game. It has been said that football has been valued as a rite of passage so that one could leave boyhood and step forward to manhood. As tough and manly as it sounds, it also has its own consequences. Players spend long hours in training so that they can improve their skills and win football games. It is not of their intention to lose. It has been said that football is a basis of masculinity and every time a team loses, embarrassment is brought forth to the losing group. One of several articles that shows this point says that "Coach Chan Gailey questioned his players' mental toughness on Monday, a day after the team's embarrassing--and near-historic--second-half collapse" (Wawrow, 2012). What is said to build character often is the source of humiliating, painful defeat.

Expense

Schools spend a large amount to cater the expenses needed for football. Finance is a sensitive topic because it involves money that has been worked hard for. Allocating the monetary expenses are a tough job and people who are in charge of it needs discernment on where and how to use it. Football has been given much attention, and they are giving away too much money for the sport. Instead of putting the expenses in a single extracurricular activity, it should be placed in programs which directly affects academics and education. As one article states, "High school football is rarely profitable" (Dent, 2011). Football just allows them to spend and put out money and rarely does it get anything back in return. This drawback has also taken the form of cash outlays that the players must make if they want to play the game (Dent).

Conclusion

Football should no longer be recognized as a Rite of Passage for a young man to enter manhood. There are several reasons why one should not partake in this event just to prove masculinity: injuries, violence, embarrassment and expense. Football is not the sole way to prove one's self worth.

Works Cited

"Boys to Men: How Boys Develop Masculinity Through Sports." *Direct Essays.* Retrieved on 13 September 2012. www.directessays.com/viewpaper/39738.html.

Dent, Mark (2011). "Special report: An Inside Look at the Finances behind HS Football in the Dallas Area" in *The Dallas Morning News.* Dallas, Texas. Retrieved on 13 October 2012. <http://www.dallasnews.com/sports/high-schools/football-news/headlines/20111117-special-report-an-inside-look-at-the-finances-behind-hs-football-in-the-dallas-area.ece>

Stevens, Tim (2012). "High School Football Brain Injuries Increasing." North Carolina. The News and Observer Publishing Company. Retrieved on 15 September 2012. <http://www.newsobserver.com/2012/04/16/2005764/high-school-football-brain_injuries.html>

Wawrow, John (2012). "Coach Gailey criticizes his players' lackluster performance in 52- 28 loss to the Pats." Lockport Union and Sun Journal Online. Lockport, New York. Retrieved on 6 October 2012. <http://lockportjournal.com/sports/x325756935/Embarrassed-Bills>

West, Peter (2010). "Why Men Play Sport" in *Manzine*, London, Germany. Retrieved on 12 October 2012. <http://www.002329aa/53ac35230f8bf0f64a256a7b0034d7af!OpenDocument>

Zamora, Jim Herron, et al.(2003). "Fear of Violence Sidelines Prep Football" Hearst Communications Inc. Retrieved on 29 September 2012, <http://www.sfgate.com/bayarea/article/FEAR-OF-VIOLENCE-SIDELINES-PREP-FOOTBALL-High-2591193.php>

Chapter 29:
A Working Exploration of Preformulations

Following is a list of 100 relatively high-register preformulations. Item "A" presents the preformulation in skeletal form, that is, without the surface-level words and phrases that would complete it and make it into a normal sentence. Sentence "B" contains the preformulation and an example of words that were added to make an acceptable surface-level sentence. Your instructor might well ask you to provide an alternate set of acceptable words that can be added to the preformulation.

In Chapter 1, you will find a fairly thorough "Introduction to Preformulation." You are urged to read that chapter before proceeding with the following exercise. You are strongly encouraged to internalize these preformulations, that is, to memorize them so that they will become accessible to you when you are writing or speaking in a formal situation. I cannot over-emphasize the importance of this process to your experience at the university.

1-A. Mention should also be made of __X__ .

1-B. Mention should also be made of <u>Selley's observation concerning reptiles</u>.

2-A. __X__ has to do with __Y__ .

2-B. <u>History</u> has to do with <u>the past</u>.

3-A. Had it not been for __X__ , __Y__ would have __V__ .

3-B. Had it not been for <u>his friend,</u> <u>Sam's experiment </u>would have<u> failed.</u>

4-A. In this paper, it is my goal to __V__ .

4-B. In this paper, it is my goal to<u> provide evidence that the survey was biased</u>.

5-A. I have tried here to show that __C__ .

5-B. I have tried here to show that <u>squirrels can be tamed</u>.

6-A. __X__ is a key element in __Y__ .

6-B. <u>Unwillingness to accept defeat</u> is a key element in <u>success</u>.

7-A. __X__ is a legitimate field of study.

7-B. <u>Sociology</u> is a legitimate field of study.

8-A. __X__ has more in common with __Y__ than with __Z__ .

8-B. <u>History</u> has more in common with <u>literature</u> than with <u>physics.</u>

9-A. This will involve at least a cursory consideration of __X__.

9-B. This will involve at least a cursory consideration of <u>anatomy</u>.

10-A. __X__ can also decrease efficiency.

10-B. <u>Fatigue</u> can also decrease efficiency.

****

11-A. In order to gain some insight into the matter, __C__.

11-B. In order to gain some insight into the matter, <u>we visited Canada</u>.

12-A. __X__ didn't fully prepare me for __Y__.

12-B. <u>Undergraduate school</u> didn't fully prepare me for <u>graduate school.</u>

13-A. During the course of __X__, Sean became ill.

13-B. During the course of <u>the graduation ceremony,</u> Sean became ill.

14-A. The data base for __X__ tended to be very narrow.

14-B. The data base for <u>his study of Brazilian frogs</u> tended to be very narrow.

15-A. With all of the attention that __X__ is now being given, __C__.

15-B. With all of the attention that <u>AIDS</u> is now being given, <u>advances have been modest</u>.

16-A. There is an urgent need to bring together __X__ and __Y__.

16-B. There is an urgent need to bring together <u>government forces</u> and <u>the rebels</u>.

17-A. To help us resolve our disagreements, __C__.

17-B. To help us resolve our disagreements, <u>we agreed to speak with negotiators</u>.

18-A. What would otherwise be __X__ is now __Y__.

18-B. What would otherwise <u>be angry silence</u> is now <u>peaceful cooperation</u>.

19-A. __C__ for as wide a variety of reasons as did __X__.

19-B. <u>Ann quit college</u> for as wide a variety of reasons as did <u>her friend</u>.

20-A. One finds such reference to __X__ in __Y__.

20-B. One finds such reference to <u>intrigue</u> in <u>books about prison life.</u>

****

21-A. Tension increased to the point that __C__.

21-B. Tension increased to the point that <u>students started fighting</u>.

22-A. We cannot say with certainty that __C__.

22-B. We cannot say with certainty that <u>no contamination occurred</u>.

23-A. Much of what we know about __X__ has come from __Y__.

23-B. Much of what we know about <u>the Milky Way</u> has come from <u>astronomers</u>.

24-A. As we have seen, __X__ permits __Y__.

24-B. As we have seen, <u>differences in the size of molecules</u> permits <u>some gasses to rise and others, to sink.</u>

25-A. We will examine some of __X__ that have __V__.

25-B. We will examine some of <u>the rockets</u> that have <u>exploded</u>.

26-A. In his essay, __X__ makes the following assertion: "__C__".

26-B. In his essay, <u>Dr. Smith</u> makes the following assertion: "<u>Language is learned behavior</u>."

27-A. But to __V__ would be an oversimplification.

27-B. But to <u>blame his parents</u> would be an oversimplification.

28-A. It is unlikely that any single one of these factors could have __V__.

28-B. It is unlikely that any single one of these factors could have <u>caused death.</u>

29-A. __X__ captured the elements of __Y__.

29-B. <u>That student's theory</u> captured the elements of <u>all of the reactions we have discussed.</u>

30-A. __X__ is not an unreasonable approach to __Y__

30-B. <u>A curfew</u> is not an unreasonable approach to <u>crime</u>.

****

31-A. This attitude led to what __X__ called __Y__.

31-B. This attitude led to what <u>the teacher</u> called <u>unbridled arrogance</u>.

32-A. __X__ was conceived as __Y__ .

32-B. <u>This shopping mall</u> was conceived as <u>an airport</u>.

33-A. __X__ does not suggest __Y__.

33-B. <u>One failure</u> does not suggest <u>the impossibility of success</u>.

34-A. As __X__ has put it, "__C__."

34-B. As <u>Roosevelt</u> has put it, "<u>We have nothing to fear but fear itself</u>."

35-A. Let us look briefly at the __X__ on which __Y__ focuses.

35-B. Let us look briefly at <u>the principle</u> on which <u>the teacher</u> focuses.

36-A. "__X__" is the label under which they were placed.

36-B. "<u>Juvenile delinquent</u>" is the label under which they were placed.

37-A. __X__ is familiar with a wide range of __Y__.

37-B. <u>A given expert witness</u> is familiar with a wide range of <u>cases in their field</u>.

38-A. While each of the above explanations accounts for __X__, __C__.

38-C. While each of the above explanations accounts for <u>different criminal acts,</u> <u>there is no way to explain the disappearance of this particular infant</u>.

39-A. __X__ has three moving parts: two __Y__ and a __Z__.

39-A. <u>The new machine</u> has three moving parts: two <u>wheels and a steering device</u>.

40-A. __X__ has shown itself to be __Adj__.

40-B. <u>The resulting data</u> has shown itself to be <u>sufficient for our purposes.</u>

****

41-A. __X__ might well be expected.

41-B. <u>Resistance to such a suggestion</u> might well be expected.

42-A. __X__ would do well to __V__.

42-B. <u>Susan LeBlanc</u> would do well to <u>study more.</u>

43-A. __X__ should lay to rest your fears of __Y__.

43-B. <u>Your performance on the tennis court this year</u> should lay to rest your fears of <u>the state championship tournament.</u>

44-A. __C1__. It does not follow, therefore, that __C2__.

44-B. <u>Alice is an honorable young lady.</u> It does not follow, therefore, that <u>she would steal money from her father in order to pay someone to take the SAT for her.</u>

45-A. This finding suggests that not only __C1__ but that __C2__.

45-B. This finding suggests that not only <u>is the sea level rising</u>, but that <u>the temperature of the water is increasing.</u>

46-A. A definitive history of __X__ remains to be written

46-B. A definitive history of <u>the suffering of the Native Americans</u> remains to be written.

47-A. __X__ is thought to __V__.

47-B. <u>Teaching very young children to play musical instruments</u> is thought to <u>promote the development of different parts of the brain.</u>

48-A. The study of __X__ is confirming the validity of __Y__.

48-B. The study of <u>Black Holes</u> is confirming the validity of <u>radical theories.</u>

49-A. There would be no purpose served if __C__ .

49-B. There would be no purpose served if <u>the teacher made the students feel inferior.</u>

50-A. __X__ determines a small set of cases to choose from.

50-B. <u>The presence of a certain combination of genes</u> determines a small set of cases to choose from.

****

51-A. If __C__, we can draw several broad conclusions.

51-B. If <u>the results are positive,</u> we can draw several board conclusions.
.

52-A. __X__ were said to have __V__ .

52-B. <u>The pewter dishes with the carefully prepared cultures</u> were said to have <u>been intentionally mislabeled.</u>

53-A. In neither __X__ is there any evidence to suggest that __C__.

53-B. In neither <u>outbreak</u> is there any evidence to suggest <u>that the disease will become epidemic.</u>

54-A. Fundamental to __X__ and to __Y__ is __Z__.

54-B. Fundamental to <u>chemistry</u> and to <u>physics</u> is <u>mathematics.</u>

55-A __X__ was poised to play a major role in determining __Y__ .

55-B. <u>The necklace</u> was poised to play a major role in determining <u>the depth of Alexander's affection for Susan.</u>

56-A. __X__ was dealt a severe blow when __C__ .

56-B. <u>Nelson's research</u> was dealt a severe blow when <u>his colleague stole all of the papers from his desk and made it known that he considered Nelson's theory his own.</u>

57-A. It is also worth mentioning that __C__ .

57-B. It is also worth mentioning that <u>Al won a Nobel Prize 20 years ago.</u>

58-A. One issue that has generated some heat is __X__ .

58-B. One issue that has generated some heat is <u>Susan's contention that Mars was inhabited 100,000 years ago.</u>

59-A. __X__, on the other hand, has claimed that __C__ .

59-B. <u>Diana's father-in-law,</u> on the other hand, has claimed that <u>his wife is the most beautiful and charming lady in all the kingdom.</u>

60-A. __X__ have come to be of __Y__.

60-B. <u>These principles</u> have come to be of <u>fundamental importance.</u>

****

61-A. __X__ adhere to a rather weaker version of this interpretation.

61-B. <u>The younger scientists</u> adhere to a rather weaker version of this interpretation.

62-A. The assumption underlying this argument is that __C__ .

62-B. The assumption underlying this argument is that <u>water expands when it freezes.</u>

63-A. This is not to say that __C__ .

63-B. This is not to say that <u>psychiatry is inherently a higher study than psychology.</u>

64-A. __X__ makes no claim to account for __Y__ .

64-B. <u>Dr. Goodall, a physicist,</u> makes no claim to account for <u>the exceptional pulsations from that star.</u>

65-A. This brings us to __X__ .

65-B. This brings us to <u>the final part of the lecture.</u>

66-A. It could be argued that __X__ are more like __Y__ than like __Z__ .

66-B. It could be argued that <u>horses</u> are more like <u>zebras</u> than like <u>bulls.</u>

67-A. We have concentrated so much on __X__ that we have neglected __Y__ .

67-B. We have concentrated so much on <u>preformulations</u> that we have neglected <u>punctuation.</u>

68-A. Since __C__ , we are justified in assuming that __C__ .

68-B. Since <u>John didn't show up at the church,</u> we are justified in assuming that <u>he has left Texas.</u>

69-A. __A__ are moving away from the idea that __C__ .

69-B. <u>Physicists</u> are moving away from the idea that <u>the universe has edges.</u>

70-A. Our primary task is __V__ .

70-B. Our primary task is <u>to clarify possible misunderstandings</u>.

****

71-A. If we accept the principle that __C1__ . it follows that __C2__ .

71-B. If we accept the principle that <u>goodness is its own reward</u>, it follows that <u>wrongdoing is its own punishment</u>.

72-A. __X__ has been held up as evidence par excellence that __C__ .

72-B. <u>Victory</u> has been held up as evidence par excellence that <u>practice makes perfect</u>.

73-A. __X__ can be recommended to any __Y__ with a need to understand __Z__ .

73-B. <u>Dr. Aldo</u> can be recommended to any <u>student</u> with a need to understand <u>math</u>.

74-A. __X__ has championed the idea that __C__ .

74-B. <u>Telleford</u> has championed the idea that <u>accomplishment is 99% perspiration</u>.

75-A. __X__ can be made to __V__ .

75-B. <u>Dogs</u> can be made to <u>perform an incredible number of different tasks</u>.

76-A. __X__ was able to demonstrate that __C__ .

76-B. <u>The teacher</u> was able to demonstrate <u>that poverty is fundamentally different in different societies</u>.

77-A. If __X__ were to __V__ , __C__ .

77-B. If <u>Joseph</u> were to <u>study and pass the test</u>, <u>his mother would be very happy</u>.

78-A. What no one can deny is that __C__ .

78-B. What no one can deny is that <u>children often learn according to what they are taught</u>.

79-A. It is generally held that __C__ ,

79-B. It is generally held <u>that animals that are apparently diseased should be isolated from animals that seem healthy</u>.

80-A. To understand why __C1__ , it is necessary that __C2__ .

80-B. To understand why <u>an employee is fired</u>, it is necessary that <u>the employer realizes much or all that is involved</u>.

****

81-A. Resistance to __X__ might well be expected.

81-B. Resistance to <u>seemingly unjust actions</u> might well be expected.

82-A. To support his hypothesis, __C__.

82-B. To support his hypothesis, <u>Robert carefully explained his evidence</u>.

83-A. This seems attributable at least in part to __X__.

83-B. This seems attributable at least in part to <u>her limited ability to speak English</u>.

84-A. As is evident in Olivia's study of __X__, her conclusions are too often reached too quickly.

84-B. As is evident in Olivia's study of <u>the reactions of mice</u>, her conclusions are too often reached too quickly.

85-A. In __X__, the distinction between __Y__ and __Z__ is often blurred.

85-B. In <u>anger</u>, the distinction between <u>right</u> and <u>wrong</u> is often blurred.

86-A. At any rate, it __V__ if Ed had lost.

86-B. At any rate, it <u>would have been just</u> if Ed had lost.

87-A. If John is out, then __X__ come into play.

87-B. If John is out, then <u>other factors</u> come into play.

88-A. This is a regular relationship such that all changes in __X__ correspond to all changes in __Y__.

88-B. This is a regular relationship such that all changes in <u>size</u> correspond to all changes in <u>shape</u>.

89-A. For the sake of argument, let us assume that __C__.

89-B. For the sake of argument, let us assume that <u>all of the animals are of the same weight</u>.

90-A. Just as __X__ can never fail to __V__, so __C__.

90-B. Just as <u>a ball thrown up</u> can never fail to <u>come down</u>, so <u>a fool can never reveal himself through silence.</u>

****

91-A. One factor that could __V__ these results was __X__ .

91-B. One factor that could <u>have affected</u> these results was <u>Beth's extreme fatigue.</u>

92-A. In a "black box" theory, there is supposedly some function that is not __V__ possible of discovery.

92-B. In a "black box" theory, there is supposedly some function that is not <u>deemed</u> possible of discovery.

93-A. The difference between nouns and verbs __V__ a major role in the study of language.

93-B. The difference between nouns and verbs <u>has played</u> a major role in the study of language.

94-A. The reported effects of __X__ were curious in the extreme.

94-B. The reported effects of <u>rock music on monkeys</u> were curious in the extreme.

95-A. This finding suggests that not only does __C1__ but that __C2__ .

95-A. This finding suggests that not only does <u>Sidney want to leave</u> but that<u> he doesn't want to come back.</u>

96-A. If __C__ , we can draw several broad conclusions.

96-B. If <u>the fish we caught have a normal level of mercury in their bodies</u>, we can draw several broad conclusions.

97-A. __X__ carries its own sense of wonder.

97-B. <u>The science of the miniscule</u> carries its own sense of wonder.

98-A. As __C__ , the above model will be modified and superseded.

98-B. As <u>research progresses,</u> the above model will be modified and superseded.

99-A. __X__ have come to be of fundamental importance.

99-B. <u>These principles</u> have come to be of fundamental importance.

100-A. __X__ might have otherwise been the case.

100-B. <u>Separation and divorce</u> might have otherwise been the case.

****

Chapter 30:
Exercises in the Academic Register

It seems that in the process of coming together and fusing with a unique reference, preformulations seem to be swiftly shunted to a different part of the metaphorical lexicon that is no longer directly associated with the meanings of those components. The unit of shunted material is thereafter integrated and used in the high register and style that is the essence of Academic Discourse. Quite conceivably, textual measurement and cognitive reflection could provide some evidence as to whether or not a particular lexical element indeed constitutes a legitimate preformulation.

Such a deliberation might indicate that the element is but another item governed entirely by syntax and operating in Academic Discourse. This determination is of secondary importance in terms of this book. What we are primarily concerned with is making a student of a second language able to recognize, understand and use in speech and writing the dialect we are calling Academic Discourse. In constructing the following exercise, it was my goal to develop such ability. Some of the boldfaced words are indeed preformulations; others are lexical items assembled in the style and with the precision of academic writing. Yet others are conversational in nature. Regardless, command and even mastery of them is much to be wished for.

It is my position that both preformulations and "preformulation-like" structures can be more effectively internalized if both are isolated. That is precisely the purpose of the 100 items that follow. It is my hope that students will become aware of these structures, able to identify them in other texts, and able to make their own lists. Then the yellow brick road to academic writing will truly have been taken.

****

Figure 15: Practice in Academic Discourse. In the sentences below, preformulations and similar structures are identified by their appearance in **bold face**. Your task is to compose another sentence in which you use the boldfaced structure and complete the sentence with your own words. Ex-1 is colloquial. Ex-2 is from Academic Discourse. In Ex-1, **"feel like ...ing"** is the target structure.

Example:

Ex-1. **Once in a while, I feel like** leaving school.
         A   B

    A. **Once in a while,** John eats food prepared in the custom of his native country.

    B. Al said that he **felt like** visiting India.

Ex-2. **I am given to understand that** **failure is not an option** in this course.
          A   **B**

    A. I am given to understand that   students who do not attend class will be dropped.

    B. The general stood up and said that **failure is not an option** in this mission.

....

1. I **have been** work**ing** on this math problem all night. Now, **I am about ready to give up**.
           A   B

A. _____

B. _____

2. This medicine **has been found** **to be safe and effective**.
                  A   B

A. _____

B. _____

3. At first glance, language **seems to have appeared** **from out of the blue**
      A   B   C

A. _____

B. _____

C. _____

4. Monkeys **can be said to** **have expressions for** predators such as snakes and eagles.
          A   **B**

A. _____

B. _____

5. He said that **the essence of music** was **harmonious sounds**.
              A   B

A. _____

B. _____

6. Chimpanzees **do not seem to possess** either words or **a system of** grammar.
               A   **B**

A. _____

B. _____

7. If that were not the case, no one would **get married**.
       A   **B**

A. _____

B. _____

8. If we are willing to face it, depression **can make us better** at **what we do**.
        A   **B**   **C**

A. _____

B. _____

C. _____

9. That chemical **is said to have played a role** in the evolution of **all living things**.
                            A   **B**

A. _____

B. _____

10. Grammar alone cannot, Coreil said, **account for** the great precision **of which**
     communication is capable.   **A**   **B**

A. _____

B. _____

11. Some scientists **are said to** deny **that which they cannot** explain.
                    A   **B**

A. _____

B. _____

12. "There is," she **said**, **"as much chance of** happiness by choosing a spouse from an
           A   **B**
     unseen list."

A. _____

B. _____

13. In a study he conducted last year, Al reported that some **plants seem to have** the
           A   **B**
     ability to communicate in some fashion with each other.

A. _____

B. _____

14. John's friend **claimed to have the ability** to **single-handedly defeat** the enemy.
                         A   **B**

A. _____

B. _____

15. The importance of cooperation was emphasized by the lecturer.
              A   **B**

A. _____

B. _____

16. The perfection of speech **may have been** **the deciding factor** in **the evolution of man**.
                                    A   B   C

A. _____

B. _____

C. _____

17. He **approved the transfer of** the two **most promising students** to the advanced class.
                  A   B

A. _____

B. _____

18. **Most of the** students **I know** **are studying** medicine or **are aspiring to do so**.
                  A   **B**   **C**

A. _____

B. _____

C. _____

19. Monkeys **spend an inordinate amount of** time **grooming one another**.
           A   B

A. _____

B. _____

20. Please, **carry out your assigned task** **whether or not** you **fully understand** the
                    A   **B**   **C**
reasoning involved.

A. _____

B. _____

C. _____

21. The terrible suffering of that war **could have been** prevented by **a word of kindness**.
                                        A   **B**

A. _____

B. _____

22. **By that time**, Al **had become intimate with** **a person for whom** he **had never felt love.**
         A   **B**   **C**   **D**

A. _____

B. _____

C. _____

D. _____

23. I **will have graduated from college** by the time **that she stops running around** .
   <u>A</u>   <u>B</u>

A. _____

B. _____

24. She **had already**   **made up** her **mind to** leave when he **didn't come home last night**.
   <u>A</u>   <u>B</u>   <u>C</u>

A. _____

B. _____

C. _____

25. Sue **ran away from home** and **sought refuge with** her aunt **who seemed to be out of a**
   <u>A</u>   <u>B</u>   <u>C</u>

Dickens novel.

A. _____

B. _____

C. _____

26. **One would think** that she **would know better than** **to get married** again..
   <u>A</u>   <u>B</u>   <u>C</u>

A. _____

B. _____

C. _____

27. He **had a good deal of** money but very little **common sense.**
   <u>A</u>   <u>B</u>

A. _____

B. _____

28. She **headed for** New York soon after graduation and **lived the rest of her life** there.
   <u>A</u>   <u>B</u>

A. _____

B. _____

29. He **was able to turn these painful experiences**--wounds, **if you will**--into valuable
   lessons.   **A**   **B**

A. _____

B. _____

30. By August, the campaign **was in full swing**, but the candidate **was shaking in his boots**.
                      A   **B**

A. _____

B. _____

31. Dr. Jose **said that once** Al's **cold was gone**, he **would be able to** play football.
                 A   **B**

A. _____

B. _____

32. **When** Jane **gets home**, she **will have to wash dishes**.
            A   **B**

A. _____

B. _____

33. **There would seem to be**   **a limit to the number of failures**   **that a given** school **can**
                 A   **B**   **C**
  experience and   **not lose all credibility**.
                 D

A. _____

B. _____

C. _____

D. _____

34. The doctor said that   he **had done everything that he could for** James.
                                         A
  "Now," he **added, "it's a matter of time."**
                 B

A. _____

B. _____

35. **It's up to her**   **whether we go or stay**.
        A   **B**

A. _____

B. _____

36. **John is not to decide**   **how many students are** needed   **to get the** football field **in**
  shape.   **A**   **B**   **C**

A. _____

B. _____

C. _____

37. The doctor said that **the patient is not to be disturbed** **for any reason whatsoever**.
                                           A   **B**

A. _____

B. _____

38. My brother **used to tell** me   **all kinds of things that were not true**.
              A   **B**

A. _____

B. _____

39. This experiment **has cost dearly**   **in terms of** money **as well as** human effort.
                 A   **B**

A. _____

B. _____

40. **Consider the following** **as an example of a polite command:** **You may** leave **if you**
         A   **B**   **C**
wish to.

A. _____

B. _____

C. _____

41. **There need be no** **rush to justice**, **as far as** Jane **is concerned**.
         A   **B**   **C**

A. _____

B. _____

C. _____

42. **I was wrong to bring it up** and **you have nothing to apologize for**.
             A   **B**

A. _____

B. _____

43. **That is to say**, **you would do well to** study more.
       A   **B**

A. _____

B. _____

44. **He is none too reliable** **when it comes to** getting up early.
       A   **B**

A. _____

B. _____

45. <u>Max **has been fired.** **So have I**</u>.
         A   **B**

A. _____

B. _____

46. <u>**To leave without**</u>   <u>**having settled the argument**</u> <u>**would be** a mistake</u>.
       A   **B**   **C**

A. _____

B. _____

C. _____

47. <u>**Don't believe that pack of lies:**</u> <u>**he wouldn't tell the truth if his soul depended on it**</u>.
         A   **B**

A. _____

B. _____

48. <u>**We're off to see** New York City</u>; <u>**would you care to come along?**</u>
        A   **B**

A. _____

B. _____

49. <u>**By the time she receives her Ph.D.,**</u> <u>**Jane will have studied** for eight years after</u>
              A   **B**
<u>undergraduate school</u>.

A. _____

B. _____

50. <u>**Sue was a failure at every sport she attempted**</u>, but <u>**she is considered a genius at**</u>
              A   **B**
<u>computers</u>.

A. _____

B. _____

51. <u>**This long-awaited book contains a larger selection**</u>   <u>**to which are added** more</u>
                 A   **B**
<u>recent poems</u>.

A. _____

B. _____

52. <u>**For more than one reason**</u> <u>**this answer is not very satisfying**</u>.
          A   **B**

A. _____

B. _____

53. <u>**When prompted by the automated tone**</u>, <u>**enter your Express Service Code**</u>.
               A   **B**

A. _____

B. _____

54. <u>**If a program stops responding**</u>, <u>**click "End Task"**</u>.
          A   **B**

A. _____

B. _____

55. <u>**You must activate your** new card immediately</u> <u>**as your old card will no longer work**</u>.
             A   **B**

A. _____

B. _____

56. <u>The soldiers **were said**</u>   <u>**to have left** the battlefield</u>.
          A   **B**

A. _____

B. _____

57. <u>**The teacher admitted that**</u> <u>**he was not familiar with**</u>   <u>**the new procedure**</u>.
          A   **B**   **C**

A. _____

B. _____

C. _____

58. <u>The book **that he bought in Soho**</u> <u>**was about**</u>   <u>**the value of passion**</u>.
          A   **B**   **C**

A. _____

B. _____

C. _____

60. <u>**Through their own experiments,**</u> <u>**students understood that** a stimulus is tied to an</u>
          A   **B**

<u>effect</u>.

A. _____

B. _____

61. <u>It remains to be seen</u>   <u>if these developments have any effect whatsoever.</u>

          A   **B**

A. _____

B. _____

62. <u>How this can be done</u>   <u>depends on financing and on</u> the motivation of teachers.

          A   **B**

A. _____

B. _____

63. <u>While there are excellent colleges here,</u>   <u>there is little interest in</u> education.

              A   **B**

A. _____

B. _____

64. <u>Education has always been highly appreciated,</u>   <u>regardless of class backgrounds</u>

              A   **B**

A. _____

B. _____

65. <u>It takes a lot of</u> practice and talent   <u>to learn to</u> play tennis <u>well</u>.

          A   **B**

A. _____

B. _____

66. <u>There is no denying that</u>   <u>adult monkeys have cognitive skills</u>

          A   **B**

   <u>that surpass those of human infants.</u>

          C

A. _____

B. _____

C. _____

67. <u>But to claim that</u>   <u>Man is cognitively inferior to monkeys</u>   <u>would be unwarranted.</u>

          A   **B**   **C**

A. _____

B. _____

C. _____

68. <u>Their impact on each other was profound:</u>   <u>they were</u> lovers, **but more,**
           A   **B**

   <u>**they were**</u> soulmates.
               C

A. _____

B. _____

C. _____

69. <u>The process</u>   <u>of which Minnis speaks</u>   <u>requires low boundaries of the self.</u>
         A1   **B**   **A2**

A1–A2. _____

B. _____

70. <u>"Give me liberty," he said,</u>   <u>in a shaky voice **with tears welling** up in his eyes.</u>
                  A   **B**

A. _____

B. _____

71. <u>**Before I had a chance** to warn the family,</u>   <u>**they had departed** on the train.</u>
                        A   **B**

A. _____

B. _____

72. <u>**This question is nowhere as pointed as in**</u> <u>**issues of guilt or innocence.**</u>
                        A   **B**

A. _____

B. _____

73. <u>**Jane takes issue with the assumption that**</u> <u>**it is a matter of black or white.**</u>
                        A   **B**

A. _____

B. _____

74. <u>**Following the dictates of human nature**</u> <u>**is not always the right way to go.**</u>
                        A   **B**

A. _____

B. _____

75. <u>**It turns out that some simple experiments**</u> <u>**yield imagination-defying results.**</u>
                        A   **B**

A. _____

B. _____

76. <u>Each of us listens to the others</u>   <u>and then does what he or she thinks is right.</u>.
         A   **B**

A. _____

B. _____

77. <u>Will Durant's family had hoped that</u>   <u>he would become a priest.</u>
         A   **B**

A. _____

B. _____

78. <u>Kushner **said the belief that**</u>   <u>a writer alone is the wellspring of</u>
              A   **B**

   <u>his or her creativity **is a debilitating myth,**</u>   <u>John-Steiner **wrote.**</u>
                  C   **D**

A. _____

B. _____

C. _____

D._____

79. <u>Compositions should have a thesis</u>   <u>and the main supports in the introduction.</u>
              A   **B**

A. _____

B. _____

80. <u>Freire **held that if social change is to occur,**</u>   <u>it must come from the oppressed</u>
                     A   **B**

A._____

B. _____

81. <u>What is impressive</u>   <u>is the manner in which</u>   <u>parallel change often occurs.</u>
              A   **B**   **C**

A. _____

B. _____

C. _____

82. <u>We aren't tempted to think that,</u>   <u>by trying hard to fly,</u>   <u>we can grow wings.</u>
                  A   **B**   **C**

A. _____

B. _____

C. _____

83. <u>Black holes are an instance of</u>   <u>extensive theory preceding evidence</u>
                   A   **B**

A. _____

B. _____

84. <u>I'm calling the police:</u> <u>they can,</u> <u>I believe,</u> <u>straighten this out.</u>
            A   **B1**   **C**   **B1**

A. _____

B1. _____

C. _____

85. <u>Living in luxury</u>   <u>is all people can think about these days.</u>
         A   **B**

A. _____

B. _____

86. <u>That is to say,</u>   <u>most thoughts are equally shallow.</u>
         A   **B**

A. _____

B. _____

87. <u>Vygotsky</u> <u>relied heavily on the ideas of Europeans and Americans</u>
                                  A

<u>in arriving at his theories</u>   <u>which have been very well received around the globe.</u>
         B   **C**

A. _____

B. _____

C. _____

88. <u>He imagined himself</u>   <u>riding through space</u>   <u>so to speak.</u>
         A   **B**   **C**

A. _____

B. _____

C. _____

89. <u>Frequented by students **and** professors,</u>   <u>The Red Cat was the cafe of choice.</u>
               A   **B**

A. _____

B. _____

90. <u>At that moment,</u>   <u>the first sound of the Freudian message echoed</u>
      A   **B**

<u>across the world.</u>
    C

A. _____

B. _____

C. _____

91. <u>Although the book is a science of morality,</u> <u>Aristotle is mindful</u>
             A   **B**

that <u>**happiness requires practical wisdom**</u> <u>in addition to philosophical virtue.</u>
              C   **D**

A. _____

B. _____

C. _____

D. _____

92. <u>If I had known of your low estimation of honor,</u> <u>I would have asked you</u> <u>to leave.</u>
             A   **B**   **C**

A. _____

B. _____

C. _____

93. <u>After Al had dated Ann for two years,</u> <u>her father inquired about</u> <u>his intentions.</u>
          A   **B**   **C**

A. _____

B. _____

C. _____

94. <u>Prudence is the habit of knowing how to act</u> <u>to secure goals in a principled way.</u>
             A   **B**

A. _____

B. _____

C. _____

95. <u>By next summer,</u> <u>I will have graduated and begun</u> <u>work on my master's degree.</u>
       A   **B**   **C**

A. _____

B. _____

C. _____

96. <u>The remainder of this article</u>   <u>will focus on a program</u>
            A   **B**

    <u>that has been implemented by your instructor.</u>
                   C

A. _____

B. _____

C. _____

97. <u>The publication of *A Nation at Risk* in 1984</u>   <u>rekindled a national debate</u>
                 A   **B**

    <u>on the "literacy crisis."</u>
        C

A. _____

B. _____

C. _____

98. <u>"I told you not to go."</u> Al's mother said,   <u>"but you went anyway.</u>
               A   **B**

    <u>That will cost you half of a month's allowance."</u>
                C

A. _____

B. _____

C. _____

99. <u>"I never want to see you again,"</u>   <u>Sue said with red cheeks</u> <u>and swollen eyes.</u>
             A   **B**   **C**

A. _____

B. _____

C. _____

100. <u>Few problems of an interpersonal nature</u>   <u>can resist concentration,</u> effort and
                    A   **B**

    <u>a sincere wish for mutual understanding.</u>
                 C

A. _____

B. _____

C. _____

Chapter 31:
Identifying and Using Preformulations in Texts

As the final step in imparting a familiarity with high register preformulations, we ask that you choose a paragraph from one of your textbooks in such fields as psychology, music, history, physics, math, biology, chemistry or business. If the book is used in college classes, very likely it will contain academic writing. Read that paragraph carefully and try to recognize in it a phrase or an expression that you have seen or heard before. There might be two or three or there might be 10 or 12. We ask that you start with no more than 10. Next to "A1" below, write the isolated structure. On line "A2," please try to construct a original sentence that contains the preformulation, with variations possible only in tense and/or number. Please use the lines on the following page and on the extra pages your instructor can provide.

Example: This sentence appeared in an essay by Lev Semenovich Vygotsky entitled "An Experimental Study of Concept Formation":

> ___*In the second place*__, this method, concentrating on the word,___
>   **A**
> ___*fails to take into account* the perception and the mental elaboration___
>   **B**
> ___of the sensory material that *give birth* to the concept.___
>   **C**

There seem to be three preformulations that are fairly easy to recognize: "in the second place," "fails to take into account,'" and "give birth."

A1. **In the second place**_____

A2. **In the second place**, I left the party because I did not want to have to talk to Jane._____

B1. **Failed to take into account**_____

B2. The professor **failed to take into account** Jack's obvious sickness._____

C1. **Give birth** _____

C2. John's cousin **gave birth** to twins during the winter vacation._____

****

Preformulations from Texts

A1. _____

A2. _____

B1. _____

B2. _____

C1. _____

C2. _____

D1. _____

D2. _____

E1. _____

E2. _____

F1. _____

F2. _____

G1. _____

G2. _____

H1. _____

H2. _____

I1. _____

I2. _____

J1. _____

J2. _____

K1 _____

K2 _____

Chapter 32:
Analyzing Academic Writing

Throughout these chapters, we have constantly stressed the importance of the thesis statement, which is the jewel in the crown of the academic term paper. In this chapter, we discuss "Written on the Wind," an essay by Stewart Brand on the digital direction of the computer in our times. There are three basic reasons why I do this: (1) To show the importance of the thesis statement, (2) to show a misuse of standard documentation, and (3) to see a negative side to the digital computerization that has swept to domination in this second decade of the 21st Century.

Having studied various parts of academic writing, we can appreciate this form in its neglect. When you see the word "unspecified" in Brand's essay, no mention was made of where or when a particular article appeared. I will attempt to point out additional shortcomings. Accidentally, I happened upon what I see as a very interesting twist concerning the thesis statement. Enter the editor. The role of the editor in most published writing--particularly academic writing--is important and usually anonymous. That is, on the staff of virtually all publications, there are usually one or more persons who make certain that the style of writing is up to par. I have served as editor and know how very necessary that role is. I have changed much of the structure of many articles with the intention of improving the flow of language and ideas. That is what an editor does.

The reason I mention this now is to help you understand how critical it is to have a well written thesis statement. In the original "Written on the Wind," I do not believe there was such a statement: I believe that the editor--whose name I do not know--realized that he or she was working with an articulate, sophisticated article which, however, did not have a pointed thesis statement. Instead, it is possible and even probable that that editor wrote one and placed it before the article, so that it might be interpreted as the missing thesis statement. Whether or not it was intended to be the statement, the following words serve as exactly that:

Thanks to the wild acceleration of technological change, digital information is being rendered irretrievable almost as soon as it is stored. Welcome to what could be the Dawn of the Digital Dark Age.

Why do I suspect that these words were added by the editor? Because in the text of the article that was archived by The Long Now Foundation, this sentence is not included. The actual essay--presented below--begins with a statement of what we have called the Old Idea. It is not until the second paragraph, that we see the cryptic: "...'digital information lasts forever--or five years, whichever comes first'." There is a clever, tongue-in-cheek quality to that phrase, but it is not of enough substance to serve as the thesis statement--which should be succinct, clear and straightforward, and does not try to be amusing. Such a clear statement is given in italic boldface above. The reason that it was not archived is that it was possibly added by an editor and was not part of the original essay. At least that is my theory.

"Written on the Wind" first appeared in the magazine *Civilization* (October/November, 1998) published by the Library of Congress (USA). Although it is not a journal, it is to be expected that the articles it publishes are sufficiently sophisticated and knowledgeable to avoid sloppy documentation. Apparently Stewart Brand was so taken with himself that he thought it unnecessary to follow elementary demands. On the other hand, while the style of writing and the content of the articles in this magazine are not perfect examples of academic writing, but they are fairly close approximations. I think that considering this article in terms of the structural analysis we have discussed will enable us to realize the validity of the following elements: old idea, transition, new idea, naming, background, evidence, and conclusion. In the running notes, where the page number is normally given, I have written "Unspecified." If Brand had specified the location and the article, readers could have checked for themselves as to whether the context was accurately represented. After all, Brand did make an effort to present evidence: it is a pity that he did not take the academic conventions more seriously. It would have helped him avoid seeming like an essentially lazy writer.

Written on the Wind
by
Stewart Brand

Thanks to the wild acceleration of technological change, digital information is being rendered irretrievable almost as soon as it is stored. Welcome to what could be the Dawn of the Digital Dark Age.

The promise has been made: "Digital information is forever. It doesn't deteriorate and requires little in the way of material media" [Grove, *Unspecified*]. So said one of the chieftains of the emerging digital age, computer-chip maker Andy Grove, the head of the Intel Corporation. Another chieftain, Librarian of Congress James H. Billington, has set about digitizing the world's largest library so that its contents can become accessible by anyone, from anywhere, forever [*Unspecified*].

But a shadow has fallen. "It is only slightly facetious," wrote RAND Researcher Jess Rothenberg in *The Scientific American*, "to say that digital information lasts forever--or five years, whichever comes first" [*Unspecified*].

Digitized media do have some attributes of immortality. They possess great clarity, great universality, great reliability and great economy--digital storage is already so compact and cheap it is essentially free. Many people have found themselves surprised and embarrassed by the reemergence of perfectly preserved e-mail or online newsgroup comments they wrote nonchalantly years ago and forgot about.

Yet those same people discover that they cannot revisit their own word-processor files or computerized financial records from ten years before. It turns out that what was so carefully stored was written with a now-obsolete application, a now-obsolete operating system, on a long-vanished make of computer, using a now-antique storage medium (where do you find a drive for a 5 1/4-inch floppy disk?).

Fixing digital discontinuity sounds like exactly the kind of problem that fast-moving computer technology should be able to solve. But fast-moving computer technology is the problem: By constantly accelerating its own capabilities (making faster, cheaper, sharper tools that make ever faster, cheaper sharper tools), the technology is just as constantly self-obsolescing. The great creator become the great eraser.

Behind every hot new working computer is a trail of bodies of extinct computers, extinct storage media, extinct applications, extinct files. Science fiction writer Bruce Sterling refers to our times as "the Golden Age of dead media, most of them with the working lifespan of a pack of Twinkies" [Sterling, *Unspecified*]. On the Internet, Sterling is amassing a roll call of their once-honored personal computer names: Altair, Amiga, Amstad, Apples I, II and III, Apple Lisa, Apricot, Atari, AT&T, Commodore, CompuPro, Cromemco, Epson, Franklin, Grid, IBM PCjr, IBM XT, Kaypro, Morrow, NEC PC-8081, NorthStar, Osborne. Sinclair Tandy, Wang, Xerox Star, Yamaha CX5M. Buried with them are whole clans of programming languages, operating systems, storage formats, and countless rotting applications in an infinite variety of mutually incompatible versions. Everything written on them was written the wind, leaving not a trace.

Computer scientist Danny Hillis [*Unspecified*] notes that we have good raw data from previous ages written on clay, on stone, on parchment and paper, but from the 1950s to the present, recorded information increasingly disappears into a digital gap. Historians will consider this a dark age. Science historians can read Galileo's technical correspondence from the 1590s but not Marvin Minsky's from the 1960s.

It's not just that file formats quickly become obsolete; the physical media themselves are short-lived. Magnetic media, such as disks and tape, lose their integrity in 5 to 10 years. Optically etched media, such as CD-ROMs, if used only once, last 5 to 15 years before they degrade. And digital files do not degrade gracefully like analog audio tapes. When they fail, they fail utterly.

Beyond the evanescence of data formats and digital storage media lies a deeper problem. Computer systems of large scale are at the core of driving corporations, public institutions, and indeed whole sectors of the economy. Over time, these gargantuan systems become dauntingly complex and unknowable, as few features are added. Old bugs are worked around with layers of "patches," generations of programmers add new programming tools and styles, and portions of the system are repurposed to take on novel functions. With both respect and loathing, computer professionals call these monsters "legacy systems." Teasing a new function out of a legacy system is not done by command, but by conducting cautious alchemic experiments that, with luck, converge toward the desired outcome.

And the larger fear looms: We are in the process of building one vast global computer which could easily become The Legacy System from Hell that holds civilizations hostage--the system doesn't really work; it can't be fixed; no one understands it; no one is in charge of it; it can't be lived without; and it gets worse every year.

Today's bleeding-edge technology is tomorrow's broken legacy system. Commercial software is almost always written in enormous haste, at ever-accelerating market velocity; it can foresee an "upgrade path" to next year's version, but decades are outside its scope. And societies live by decades; civilizations, by centuries.

Digital archivists thus join an ancient lineage of copyists and translators. The process, now as always, can introduce copying errors and spurious "improvements," and can lose the equivalent of volumes of Aristotle. But the practice also builds the bridge between human language eras--from Greek to Latin, to English, to whatever's next.

Archivist Howard Besser [*Unspecified*] points out that digital artifacts are increasingly complex to revive. First there is the viewing problem--a book displays itself, but the contents of a CD-ROM are invisible until opened on something. Then there's the scrambling problem--the innumerable ways that files are compressed and, increasingly, encrypted. There are interrelationship problems--hypertext or website links that were active in the original, now dead ends. And translation problems occur in the way different media behave--just as a photograph of a painting is not the same experience as the painting, looking through a screen is not the same as experiencing an immersion medium, watching a game is not the same as playing it.

Gradually a set of best practices is emerging for ensuring digital continuity: Use the most common file formats; avoid compression where possible; keep a log of changes to a file; employ standard metadata; and make multiple copies and so forth.

Another approach is through core standards, like the DNA code in genes or written Chinese in Asia, readable through epochs while everything changes around and through them. The platform-independent programming language called Java boasts the motto "Write Once, Run Anywhere." One of Java's creators, Bill Joy, asserts that the language "is so well specified that if you write a simple version in Java, it becomes a Rosetta Stone. Aliens, or a sufficiently smart human, could eventually figure it out because it's an implementation of itself" [*Unspecified*]. Exercise is always the best preserver. Major religious works are impressively persistent because each age copies, analyzes and uses them. The books live on and are kept contemporary by frequent use.

Since digital artifacts are quickly outnumbering all possible human users, Jaron Lanier recommends employing artificial intelligencies to keep the artifacts exercises through centuries of forced contemporaneity [*Unspecified*]. Still, even robot users might break continuity. Most reliable of all would be a two-path strategy: To keep a digital artifact perpetually accessible, record the current version of it on a physically permanent medium, such as silicon disks microetched by Norsam Technologies in New Mexico, then go ahead and let users, robot or human, migrate the artifact through generations of versions and platforms, pausing from time to time to record the new manifestation on a Norsam disk. One path is slow, periodic and conservative; the other, fast, constant and adaptive. When the chair of use is eventually broken, it leaves a permanent record of the chair until then, so the artifact can be retrieved to begin the chain anew.

How can we invest in a future we know is structurally incapable of keeping faith with its past? The digital industries must shift from being the main source of society's ever-shortening, attention span to becoming a reliable guarantor of long-term perspective. We'll know that shift has happened when programmers begin to anticipate the Year 10,000 Problem, and assign five digits instead of four to year dates. "01988" they'll write, at first frivolously, then seriously.

Structural Analysis of Magazine Article
"Written on the Wind"
by
Clyde Coreil

I. Title: "Written on the Wind"

II. Thesis Statement (attributed to editor): "Thanks to the wild acceleration of technological change, digital information is being rendered irretrievable almost as soon as it is stored. Welcome to what could be the Dawn of the Digital Dark Age."

III. Detail from Old Idea, which is that digitization is enormously beneficial:

A. Quotation: "Digital information is forever. It doesn't deteriorate and requires little in the way of material media."

B. Reference to Billington, who wants to digitize the world's largest library to make it more accessible.

IV. Transition to New Idea: "But a shadow has fallen. 'It is only slightly facetious to say that digital information lasts forever--or five years, whichever comes first'."

V. New Idea: (See item II above. The thesis statement is given first, apparently because it was thought by the author or the editor to be new and to catch the attention and interest of the reader. See also Coreil's suggestion in the note above.)

VI. Background: "Digitized media do have some attributes of immortality. They possess great clarity, great universality, great reliability and great economy--digital storage is already so compact and cheap it is essentially free." This paragraph can be considered background because it explores the "Old Idea."

VII. Transition from "background" to "naming" the categories of support for the New Idea: "Yet those same people discover [that the data cannot be retrieved].

VIII. 1st Piece of Supporting Evidence: (Possible Subhead: Self-Obsolescing Technology)

"...fast moving computer technology is the problem....[it] is...self-obsolescing." The following paragraph presents evidence of this: "Behind every new working computer is a trail of bodies....Everything written on them waswritten on the wind, leaving not a trace."

IX. Transition from 1st Support to 2nd Support: "Beyond the evanescence of data formats and digital storage media lies a deeper problem."

X. 2nd Support: (Possible Subhead: Patches on Patches)

    A. "Computer systems of large scale....become...dauntingly complex and unknowable, as new features are added...with layers of 'patches'...that converge toward the desired outcome."

    B. Transition from (A) to (C) in 2nd support: "And the larger fear looms...."

    C. "We are in the process of building one vast global computer...that doesn't really work...and it gets worse every year."

XI. 3rd Support: (Possible Subhead: Avoiding Disaster)

"Commercial software is almost always written in enormous haste." As a result, "digital artifacts are increasingly difficult to revive....The contents CD-ROM are invisible until opened on something." Other problems involve compression, encrypting and links that no longer lead anywhere.

XII. Statement of Alternatives: (Possible Subhead: Avoiding Disaster)

"Gradually a set of best practices is emerging for ensuring digital continuity...."

       1. Use common file formats
       2. Avoid Compression
       3. Keep a log of changes to a file
       4. Java is self-explanatory
       5. Use the files frequently
       6. Save data periodically

XIII. Conclusion:

    A. Presentation of detail ("Digital information is forever."

    "How can we invest in a future we know is structurally incapable of keeping faith with its past."

    B. Brief statement of possible solution: "The digital industries must shift from being the main source of society's ever-shortening attention span to becoming a reliable guarantor of long-term perspective."

    C. Second reference to detail: Mention of Y2K problem.

###

Note: The above is presented solely as instruction in analysis, and not as instruction related to the storage of information on computers. Coreil

Chapter 33:
Assignments

At this point, I will explain the procedure that I follow in my classes. During the first half of the semester, my students construct a short (1,000-word) "Practice Term Paper" with a topic similar to "Boxing Should Be Banned." The topic of this semester's practice paper was "Football Should Be Banned from School Sports." A sample can be found in Chapter 28: it is provided to give you an idea of what your completed "real" and final term paper will look like. Your project will include an Appendix immediately preceding the bibliography or "Works Cited." The categories of evidence will be similar, as will the introduction, background, and conclusion. It is of great importance that you realize that in this course, most of what we study will be demonstrated in this Term Paper project. One of main textbooks will be the present one entitled *Term Papers and Academic Writing: A Classroom Text*. Your instructor will probably test you on the contents of this book.

First Things First

The first thing that you will do in approaching this Practice Paper is find evidence that is relevant to our first category, which is "Danger of Physical Injury." You already know that the

Old Idea is that football is an excellent preparation for the transition to manhood. And your New Idea is that football should be banned. You also know that there are about four categories of evidence you will offer in support of your Thesis Statement. Among those might be the following:

(1) Injuries to limbs and—possibly more critical—to the head and brain,
(2) The learning of the objectionable lesson that violence can lead to winning,
(3) The place of such an expensive sport in an educational institution, and
(4) The often considerable cost to individual students of participating in that sport.

Please turn to Chapter 26: Writing in the Right Voice—Formal vs. Informal. You will find there detailed instructions on how to proceed with these assignments. What you are doing in this first task is developing the first category of evidence. Later, we will go back to writing the Introduction and providing the Background. The reason why we go immediately to the first piece of evidence is to help insure that you are thinking of these papers--practice and final--as highly structured arguments and not as ongoing narratives that do not place primary importance on discrete categories, objective evidence and logical structure. Study the "Skeletal Outline of Academic Paper" in Chapter 17 for information on structure and length. The first assignment is part 5 of "Evidence." I will assign the second part of this Practice Paper one week before it is due.

To complete the first assignment, you are free to use whatever kind of support that you wish--the internet, the library, interviews, sports magazines, newspapers, television broadcasts, radio broadcasts, or anything else you can dream up. <u>You must reach out for evidence beyond</u>

the internet: failure to do so will adversely affect your final grade. This evidence must be real and not imaginary, and you must indicate the source and other information on the Research Report form you can find in Chapter 24. (I will provide you with an extra copy of this form that you can copy it without bending or breaking your copy of this book.) Possibly, I will ask you to staple that form to at most three pages of printout or duplication.

We will proceed in this fashion until all major sections are complete. I will comment on the completed, letter-perfect, typed "Practice Term Paper" which will constitute part of the Mid-Term Exam. During the second half of the semester, you will choose a different topic from the 70 suggested in Chapter 19. If you wish to suggest a topic not from the 70, your instructor will have to approve it. You will develop your own original term paper according to exactly the structure and mode of presentation you followed for the practice project. This "Final Term Paper" will be due approximately two weeks before the Final Exam. My first examination of your paper will be made to insure that the format is basically the same as the one presented in this book.

Nota Bene: A grade of "C-" or below ranges from very poor to unacceptable. A grade of "C" or better is satisfactory. A grade of "B" is good. A grade of "B+" is something you might like to write home about. A grade of "A-" and "A" is excellent and is reserved for students who have demonstrated noteworthy initiative and have performed according to very high standards.

Subsequent Assignments

The second assignment will probably be to write a brief account of the background as described in Chapter 21. An important part of this assignment is your indicating clearly where you found the information--that is, your source or sources. If you are quoting a sentence, you should indicate immediately after the quotation mark and before the period the name of the author or authors and the page or pages in this fashion. You will put complete information in the bibliography, presented on the last page of your paper. If you would like to use this text as a source, you are welcome to do so. For example, if you wish to quote from this text, you should do as in Figure 16

****

Figure 16. Examples of 'Running Notes' and Bibliographic Entry: In the MLA system, the parenthetical or "running" note usually gives the last name of the author and the page number(s) from which the quotation is taken. An alternative is to indicate the year of publication after the name. Here, the quotation and running note are in "A" and the entry in the bibliography is in "B."

A. "An important part of this assignment is your indicating clearly where you found the information--that is, your source or sources" (Coreil, 155).

B. Coreil, Clyde (2013). *Term Papers and Academic Writing: A Classroom Text.* West Conshohocken, PA: Infinity Publishing.

****

If the source is the internet and no author is given, you will put the first important word in the title (not "the" or "a"). The bibliography--sometimes called "Works Cited" or "References"--is always arranged alphabetically and in reverse or "hanging" indentation. In <u>regular</u> indentation, the first word of a paragraph is pushed in five spaces and the other sentences are flush left. In "<u>reverse</u> indentation," the first word of the citation is flush left and the other sentences are pushed in five spaces. The main purpose of reversing the indentation is to make the last name of the author or the first important word of the title easy to find.

The preceding is part of the documentation method as called for by *A Guide to MLA Documentation* which we will follow in most ways (Trimmer). Two ways in which we will not follow the *Guide* are in (1) single spacing between lines of the bibliography and in (2) using italics for main titles in that bibliography. For many years, students have been able to use italics on the computer. The underlining of titles was popular in the days of the typewriter which was not capable of making letters in the italics font. My recommendation for single spacing both in the text and in the bibliography has to do with coherence of presentation and reading: I find it disconcerting to see the design element of spacing between lines virtually lost in a term paper of 1,500 or more words. Please follow your instructor's directions regarding this matter.

For simple essays and other forms of short writing, I recommend double spacing between lines. Other methods of presenting documentation can be found in publications of the American Psychological Association (APA). Normally, we will use the MLA style.

Appendix

Note: The following article is reprinted with permission from *The 'X' Point: Where Imagination is Lost* (2011) to develop in greater detail our contention that preformulation is indeed a structural and fundamental part of all languages.

****

Preformulations:
A Needed Sea Change in Language Instruction
by
Clyde Coreil

New Jersey City University
coreil@erols.com, ccoreil@NJCU.edu, imagination@NJCU.edu

2039 Kennedy Boulevard
Jersey City, New Jersey 07305
USA

Two activities—creative writing and linguistics—describe Dr. Raymond Clyde Coreil. Carnegie Mellon University afforded him an M.F.A in theater/playwriting and two of his best years leading roundabout to a Ph.D. in linguistics from the City University of New York. Author of many plays and poems, he is now working on The Xanadu Sea and Other Short Stories, *many of which are set in his native Deep South.*

Editor's Note: *The editor of this book and the author of this article are one and the same person, who has worked fairly extensively in both imaginative and academic writing. He observes that although different sets of neurons are probably involved, both sets fall under the same rubric of the imagination. He considers that rubric to preside equally in science, philosophy, psychology, art, and humane letters. More precisely, whenever solutions are passionately sought, there is fertile ground for the imagination.*

Introduction

The structures I will call "preformulations" have certainly been noticed and written about extensively: e.g., Pawley and Syder (1983) call them "lexicalized sentence stems," p. 191. Nattinger and DeCarrico (1992), "lexical phrases"; Lewis (1993), "prefabricated formulaic items" (p. 121); Yorio (undated draft), "conventionalized language," and Coreil (1992), "supralexicals." Van Lancker (1987) refers to nonpropositional formulaic speech, and proceeds to offer what is still the most thorough and insightful analysis of its role in language. She is not concerned with language teaching, and she does not point out that these can be thought of as lexical, structural, conceptual, intonational, and "identificational" in nature.* Rather she modestly asserts at the end of her article that the "properties and attributes indicated for nonpropositional speech are meant to be suggestive only" (p. 104). In my opinion, she does far more than simply suggest: she makes what I consider a compelling case for considering formulaic speech as fundamental to language as is syntax. I intend for the present article to do little more than propose a footnote concerning the unfortunate neglect of formulaic speech—or "preformulations"—in the language classroom. I will attempt to cite coherent reasons for doing so, and for suggesting yet another term that I hope captures the function I have in mind. I will refer to an implementation of this in the appendix. (* In order to more securely ground the notion of preformulations, I also make reference to a wider scope of the structures in the endnote.)

I believe that preformulations constitute up to—and perhaps even more than—one-half of all acceptable expressions that can be represented at all registers according to syntactic rules. Part of this vast sea of expressions is accounted for by the power of preformulations to have priority over syntax (see below) and to be used recursively, an example of which follows: A+B=C. A *...is thought to...*; B *... ...play a major role in...*. C = Love *is thought to play a major role in* marriage. Both A and B are independent preformulations that can be combined with each other to yield C, an acceptable third structure. There is little question that preformulations abound, yet they are neglected in virtually all language instruction.

As a result, proficiency is retarded and comes about as this mass of structures at best slowly, randomly and largely unconsciously enter the student's lexicon of the Native or Non-Native language being acquired. I think that a far better approach would be to introduce preformulations as a vital part of language from the very first class. This would seem to represent the "sea change in language teaching" that is mentioned with precious little modesty in the title. Preformulations stare every language teacher in the face, yet these structures are presented basically as anomalies because they lack the holy permutability of blessed syntax. These are not primarily "syntactic structures" (Chomsky, 1957), yet they seem to constitute an equally fundamental part of language.

When two or more identical lexical items occur several times in identical sequence, they will likely develop a new single identical semantic value and will likely constitute a "preformulation." This particular linguistic element is indeed a newly formed lexeme that is related to part of the first and to part of the second item, but they—or rather "it"--will apparently move into a new part of the brain (cf. Van Lancker, p. 101). In other words, the preformulation— or somewhat more properly the "lexical preformulation"—which is primarily what this article will deal with--will access and express a new concept. Examples of the 40,000+ preformulated lexical units that probably exist in English include: "go to sleep," "get married to," "have a nervous breakdown," "the show must go on," "we will get to that in a second," "mention should also be made of," "this is not to say that," "run that by me again," "a stitch in time saves nine," "buckle down," "turn him in," "turn it on," "turn him on," "by the way," "lost cause," "elbow grease," "pass muster," "don't get me started on that," and "perish the thought."

Preformulations include idioms, proverbs, metaphors, expressions considered trite and others prestigious, syntactically anomalous constructions, and any number of grammatically approved or disapproved expressions of virtually any length. If the specific lexical items recur in the same order, and if they do not vary except for tense and number—then they have very likely undergone the thoroughly legitimate process of preformulation and exist in the speaker's lexicon as a new lexical item. As a result, non-native speakers often superimpose preformulations from their own language and say things like, "*John was married with Jane" instead of "John got married to Jane."

It is most unfortunate that students are not taught both the principle of preformulations and given graded lists of actual preformulations as such in classes in both the Native and Non-Native language. The structure "this is not to say that" would obviously not be suitable for early placement on our hypothetical list. Conversely, "go to sleep" would--instead of *"start sleeping." The onerous job of preparing materials for classroom use has not yet been undertaken. Perhaps the most time-consuming task would be the compilation of a "Dictionary of Preformulations" in a given language that would specify the level of register at which the preformulation in question might best be introduced.

Treading the Yellow Brick Road

Unless we fully recognize what we have <u>not</u> been doing, we will resist that change and continue to dismiss it when and if it is brought up. Our students will continue making halting progress as they tread a yellow brick road that is desperately in need of repair. We will look closely at the preformulation "go to sleep" in just a moment. I would, however, like to begin by making it clear that I do not think that "preformulations" are bound by register, dialect, variety, or any related features of a given language. Rather, the preformulative process seems to be an integral part of all languages. One other part is syntax, which yields when there is a conflict: e.g., "perish the thought," which does not seem to follow any syntactic pattern. "Perish" is intransitive—one cannot "perish" anything. Also, "perish" can be construed only as second person, but this notion cannot be conjugated: *He perishes the thought."

Restatement of Definition

Preformulations are fixed, recurring patterns of lexical items that merge, move and acquire, upon preformulation, a unique semantic value. Let us look more closely at this three-part process. Two or more lexemes undergo a metaphor-like combination of some of their semantic features (the merging) and literally take up residence in a new place in the brain (the moving). The lexicon thereupon increases by a factor of at least one its ability to conceive of and manipulate this new meaning (the acquisition).

Lexical and Structural Preformulations

A seemingly related aspect of this largely semantic process is the structural change that sentences undergo in order to stress certain elements and otherwise do things like move phrases and clauses around for the sake of proximity to other elements. One example of such a "structural preformulation" is the move to the subject position of noun phrases such as the following: "<u>That she is profoundly depressed</u> is obvious." Another example is the use of "that" as a marker of parallels: "I am told <u>that</u> he is an important man, <u>that</u> he is very busy, and <u>that</u> he is working on a critical report." Another is the use of "such that" to relate clauses: "His daily activities are <u>such that</u> he rarely has time to sleep." Yet another is the use of the infinitive as subject: "<u>To eat</u> would have made Harry less irritable." The use of "so" as a pro-verb is also relevant: I asked him <u>to leave</u>, and he <u>did so</u>.

In structures such as the preceding, there is little lexical activity: rather, the fixing occurs at another, probably deeper level more closely related to syntax. In both cases, the particular phenomenon in question is the ability to access and express the unique formula that yields the desired semantic notion. This is possibly most apparent in the case of Academic Discourse. There, one must be extraordinarily able to do these things—i.e., have access to, use and manipulate both lexical and structural preformulations—in order to be considered a relatively sophisticated native or native-like speaker.

Fossilization

The lexical item "fossilization" has added, to its list of semantic features pertaining to language, one of negativity. When a student of some second language repeatedly uses the same unacceptable form of a construction, we call it an instance of "fossilization" that is to be corrected and its constituent elements returned to their syntactic freedom as soon as possible. An example of a structure most teachers would call fossilized is the following: *"Where you studied when you in homeland country?" On the other hand most of us would never dream of classifying as fossilized a highly acceptable construction like *"He should have been made to realize that that sort of behavior is by no means acceptable."* Yet there is present the same sort of lexical fixing in both underlined structures. If students were introduced to preformulations as we are defining them, it might help them understand why the teacher says that one string of recurring words is unacceptable, but another is acceptable because it is a preformulation--although many preformulations are—sui generis—not in keeping with the rules of syntax: "John has to put a stop to this kind of behavior" (*"John always wants to take a stop out of more acceptable behavior").

Preformulative Deviation

Deviation from or avoidance of more direct and straightforward expressions does indeed seem to be a fundamental characteristic of a great many preformulations: e.g., "go to sleep" instead of "*start sleeping" and "Let's make a run for it" instead of "?Let's run to that safe place." This would seem to imply a purpose to the deviation—possibly a mnemonic which would provide a tabular signal to the language processing device that the structure is not to be interpreted syntactically but holistically according to specified memory. If this should be the case, it would be interesting evidence that language is not only of hierarchic structure because the very concept of hierarchies cannot tolerate a completely different uber-system which would require activation based on the simultaneous presence of both aberration and memory. The latter explanation is, in fact, not hierarchic but agglomerative. Perhaps language would be more accurately conceived as balls of different systems stuck together by some sort of cognitive glue—coordinated by a yet unnamed function. Needless to say, this is speculation.

Specialized Preformulations

In the higher register of Academic Discourse, the ability to handle lexical and structural preformulations clearly seems to have beneficial effects on the perceiving, comprehension and relating of involved sets of technical relationships. Knowing a specific preformulation in a field like law or medicine helps us relate it to another, probably equally involved preformulation. For example, a building normally *"runs with the land"*; i.e., it is part of the inheritor's good fortune.

146

The ability to comprehend and manipulate *runs with the land* in different contexts such as the deteriorated condition of such a building is part and parcel of the training of a good lawyer.

Although the "Grammar of Medicine" or the "Grammar of Law" is rarely spoken of, fluency in such a Grammar is assumed by fellows in either discipline. In other words, upon the process of specialized preformulation, speakers enhance their ability to perceive and conceive relationships in the realm of Academic Discourse or Professional "Jargon" that before might have eluded them. It is possible that they felt the need to express a particular idea that had been "kidnapped" by a singular preformulation. The chances of arriving at that particular formulation via logic, syntax or whatever are next to impossible, and even those low chances diminish as more words are used.

> ***1st Year Law Student:*** *It's when a building is inherited because it was built on the land that itself was inherited regardless of when the building was built, and the liability involved is not decreased because it was already on the land when the land was inherited.*

> ***Experienced Lawyer: That building is said to "run with the land." Got it?***

Similar and probably far more dramatic increases take place in other registers as relevant preformulations occur

Preformulations Trump Syntax

The preformulation "Perish the thought" is anomalous but perfectly acceptable. It is an example of how these structures ultimately decide whether a given expression is to be considered acceptable and occur at all levels of speech from those used in locker rooms to those used in the speech and writing of the highest academic discourse. Usually, they are in accord with syntax, but "preformulations" win out when there is a conflict. "For example, consider, "Zip a dee doo dah, zip a dee ay," a preformulation with scant reference to syntax. Yet if we try a variation such as "*Zoop a do dah dee, zoon u der den" it will be clearly unacceptable.

Negation of Synonymy

This "Zip a dee" context is useful in pointing out that one result of the full implementation of the theory of preformulations is that the notion of synonymy is negated. No lexical item or preformulation has the same set of semantic features as another. One of several reasons why "big" is not the same as "large" is that the latter is used in indicating the size of clothing, whereas "big" has the feature of insufficient formality for that purpose. This principle that <u>language rejects synonymy</u> extends to the acceptability of "go to sleep" and the unacceptability of "*start sleeping" which might seem to occupy an even higher berth of register. Perhaps it is that similarity, however, which activates the locking out of one of the expressions.

Go To Sleep vs. Start Sleeping

Let us continue with what is probably one of the most widely used preformulations in the English language: "go to sleep." In the Oxford University corpus of actual expressions, this particular structure was used some 150,000 times compared to not even a single usage of "*start sleeping," which needs an asterisk to indicate that it is not acceptable although there is no obvious syntactic deviation involved. I can "start writing," "start cooking," "start walking" and start any number of activities: yet I cannot "*start sleeping."

You might say that it is the internal relationship of the lexical features of "sleeping" that prevents usage of "start" plus "sleeping." I think that your argument would be wrong, but I will gladly offer another example. I would not have to look very far because there is an enormous number of other instances of two or more words that are always used together with changes only in tense and sometimes number but not in the specifics of the exact constituent lexical items or the sequence in which they occur. If we consider "go fishing" we find another basic characteristic of preformulations: they "kidnap" or capture a precise meaning and will not share that meaning with any other phrase or construction. For example, "I fished" does not refer to the broader experience of "went fishing." The structure "go to fish" implies purpose plus not necessarily completed action: I may have gone to the river to fish but found that it was severely polluted so I turned around and went back home. In other words, synonymy is "a dream and folly of expectation" (Sir Thomas Browne, referring to life without death), a literate, high-register preformulation.

Cut in Two

Another example is one that I actually heard on Public Broadcasting Radio several years ago. A sophisticated announcer who spoke English as a native language was interviewing a Frenchman who spoke English as a second language. The gentleman from France was a lawyer who had to watch as his convicted client was executed by Guillotine. I will try to reproduce that dialogue:

> *Frenchman:*   *I was shocked. I watched my client being cut in two.*
> *Announcer:*   *You mean he was decapitated.*
> *Frenchman:*   *Yes. That's what I said. His body was cut in two.*
> *Announcer:*   *He lost his head.*
> *Frenchman:*   *(irritated) Yes. I just told you!*

The announcer went on to other things without expressing the miscommunication. The preformulation "to cut in two" has the feature: to divide in roughly <u>equal</u> portions. The poor client's body was not divided into roughly equal portions: his head was far smaller than the remaining torso, arms and legs. The announcer discretely attempted to point this out by using the word "decapitated," but the Frenchman thought that the Guillotine divided the man into two discrete parts and therefore that the use of the preformulation "cut in two" was exactly correct. He was mistaken—he had not been aware that this expression includes the semantic feature "equal." This example illustrates the fact that unless the student of a second language learns or subliminally acquires many if not all of the features of a particular preformulation, he will make

148

mistakes. Apparently, in his native language, he acquires this awareness cumulatively by seeing and hearing countless discrete preformulations used with great precision by adults and older children. Unfortunately, in the second language classroom, teachers usually fail to discuss preformulations, possibly because they were not discussed by their own teachers of applied linguistics and pedagogical methodology.

The Sea Change

This is precisely the situation that I wish to start a sea change over, having the temerity to state that this seems to be a big, basic deficiency in language teaching. I expect the "Brooklyn Raspberry" but hope for something more constructive. After attempting to ground this hypothesis in slightly more formal linguistics, I will give an example of how I am using preformulations in the teaching of academic writing to "advanced" ESL students. This is quite a job, considering that Academic Discourse consists largely of very high register preformulations that are virtually never used in run-of-the-mill conversation or even popular novels. Yet I like to think that a quantum leap can be made or at least approximated.

Searching for a Term

The linguistic structures we are looking at have been called—among many other things— "products of frozen syntax," "chunks," "lexical phrases," and "lexicalized sentence stems." But these wouldn't do. I needed a name that would include all multiple-item units that do not vary but recur in the same order when triggered by or triggering one, particular precise situation; AND that would have sole linguistic access to that situation and to the expressing of that situation. There are two locks, one on each side of the door between access and expression.

I find the process of locking and unlocking that door of great importance to the structure, not only of language, but of much human thought itself, particularly to those processes that are formulated and used as recursive units in constructing more complex ideas. Because my focus was on language, the term I needed would also have to approximate syntax, semantics and lexicon in scope, but that would signify something very different. "Preformulation," I believe, meets all of those requirements and includes but extends far beyond idioms, proverbs and cliches. It does not refer to the difference between speech and language, or that it applies to phrases more than clauses. Nor does it imply necessary derivation from syntactic structures. It does refer to a "form" existing before, and it does refer to a process. Also, it does not now exist as an independent lexical item, so the problem of ambiguity is diminished.

Non-Systematic

While syntax is a rule-governed <u>system</u> that is usually applied to communication, individual preformulations are far less involved in systematic constructs. Generally, they are acquired one by one, but are of great importance in determining whether a specific lexical formulation will be deemed acceptable, particularly with reference to specific situations. My basic contention is that the concept of "lexicon" consists of what are usually considered (1) single lexical items that can be put together according to systematic syntactic rules, as well as (2) specific preformulations that usually follow little or no system of rules. Interestingly, two of the few rules of construction that preformulations often seem to follow is: **"Stray from syntactic and semantic rules"** and **"Use metaphor."** An example of this is the somewhat bizarre "take a taxi" instead of the more explicit "?ride in a taxi."

Space dictates that I limit myself to suggesting (A) that preformulations exist as I define them, (B) that language is agglomerative and not (primarily) hierarchical, (C) that both syntax and preformulations evolve, and (D) that preformulations are useful in the study of the structure and history of language itself. More broadly but briefly, we will point out their relevance to (E) neurolinguistic considerations, to (F) code-switching, and finally to (G) all primate thought.

Preformulations and Change

Because there seems to be more change in a dynamic system over the years, we might expect less change in preformulated structures. For example, although the meaning of "spic" and "span" as independent lexical items has faded, a great many people know that, as a preformulation, "spic and span" means that everything is clean and in its place. Accordingly, we tend to assume that preformulations endure longer than their constituents, which seems the case with "auld lang syne." This could have implications for the historical relationship between languages. Also interesting is a comparison of "translated" preformulations which have a one-to-one relationship with preformulations in another language. An example is "el otro dia" in Spanish and "the other day" in English, both of which I would classify as preformulative. In both languages,"el otro dia" and "the other day" do not refer primarily to one day instead of another—e.g., to Wednesday instead of Saturday--but to "the recent past."

Many other expressions are preformulative in one language and not the other. For example, in Spanish the word "tomer" means "to drink" or "to take something with one" as in "He tomado el libro" or "I took the book with me." "He tomado la tableta dos veces por dia" means "I took the tablet twice a day." Directly translated, that would be *"I drank the tablet twice a day." Which is extremely confusing if the speaker does not know that the preformulation in Spanish "tomer la tableta" cannot be expressed in English by "*drink the tablet": We cannot "drink" tablets in English; we have to "take" tablets. This is very much like the French lawyer who saw his client being "cut in two" by the Guillotine. The enormous number of preformulations generally equals the enormous number of miscommunications that can occur if preformulations are not taught in second language classrooms. Yet at present, "preformulations" are virtually always considered "interesting anomalies" that pale before syntactic structures.

A related idea is that a preformulation will virtually always be preferred over an almost identical expression although there is apparently little or no semantic difference or grammatical deficiency. An example of this is the frequently heard "go to sleep" and the never encountered "*start sleeping." Without the argument on preformulations, this pair—"go to sleep" and "*start seeping"--represents quite a conundrum. Other quotidinal preformulations are "once upon a time," "do no harm," "when it comes to X," "boy crazy," "to be a complete mess," "despite X's efforts," "day laborer," "show me the money," "take a call," "ready or not, here I come," "Davy Jones' locker," "to keep 'em coming" (and probably not "*to keep them coming,") "do or die," "give 'em the slip," "to whistle in the dark," "to die trying," "to give up," "to calm down," "to leave Person X for Person Y" and "to be reluctant to part with." For a native speaker, such preformulations seem perfectly natural. For many non-native speakers, however, each preformulation is a trap into which he or she will probably fall into—as did our French lawyer.

Happy Days but not *Happy Weeks

Yet another example is "Happy days are here again." This is the first line of a political song that once became popular as an expression of hope regarding the return of the Democratic Party in the USA. A Republican "wouldn't be caught dead" whistling that song. The "de facto" Confederate anthem *Dixie* is even more verboten, forbidden and a treasonous breach of "Political Correctness" for a Yankee to even hum, much less "find on his lips." Although some may not understand how a day can be happy but a week can't, syntax generally allows us to put the rest of these words together in a meaningful combination. But some other operation was necessary in order for "Happy days are here again" to become an auditory icon of hope in a complex situation that was tied to "widespread poverty," dislocation and suffering. What I am suggesting is that the needed operation which syntax lacked was provided by the phenomenon of preformulation. This process continues daily at a stunning pace as the semantic need for new yet precise names, concepts, entities, procedures, etc. demand a reference in the lexicon, which apparently usually abhors the un-nameable.

Preformulative Shunting

Let us consider *Happy Days* more closely. After syntax had enabled us to make basic sense of this string of sounds, we added--in the process of preformulation--the meaning as it occurred in a certain social context. After a couple of repetitions, the entire sentence-- "Happy days are here again"--seems to have changed identity from a well formed syntactic string: it became accessible as a pre-formed structure WITH a highly specific and precise meaning. We might refer to this process of uniting previously discrete lexical items as "preformulative shunting" to another part of the brain. Similar processes have occurred with phrases and clauses or indeed even with our nonsensical string "Zip a dee doo dah, zip a dee ay" which continues with, "My oh my oh what a wonderful day." The first preformulation here is "Zip a dee doo dah, zip a dee ay." These were no more than nonsense sounds: there was no semantic content there— at least not until the song became popular and the nonsensical string was transformed into a preformulation. The original components still make no sense. In other words, the process occurred with nonsense syllables which became semantically meaningful as a result of preformulative shunting.

Before this transformation occurred to "happy days are here again," it seems likely that each word had been independently stored in separate parts of the brain. The semantic charge, however, caused these five words to move or be shunted to a SINGLE location in that mental organ. Now the parts—**Happy+days+are+here+again**—became a single whole, a single entity. AND that entity yields access to a single notion—a set of difficulties related to poverty in a precise context. If I want to express that precise notion, I have to use these words exactly as they have undergone preformulation. I cannot get the meaning with, "Pleasant times have returned" or "Trouble-free days are coming again." I have frozen not only the syntax and the exact lexical constituents--I have also elbowed the one-dimensional lexicon into the background and added a deeply enriching, multi-dimensional semantic foreground.

These are closely related to the two parts of language that I referred to earlier: One is the mechanism of syntax; the other is the shunting and enfolding of level after level of meaning. According to Loraine Obler in conversation and to Van Lancker (p. 103), people suffering from several types of aphasia seem to retain a disproportionately large part of their ability to recognize and use preformulated language while losing much of the ability to use syntax. This might mean that preformulation involves an older part of the human brain—possibly the limbic system. If this is true, of course, the speculation regarding shunting would be supported. Also, it would dovetail with the evolution of preformulations, as we will see.

Although it is somewhat similar to counting dancing angels, I do not see the relationship between preformulations and syntax as well represented in a kind of continuum. Ladies are not usually said to doff their hats to persons or conventions, yet Van Lancker seems to be doing just that in the following sentence: "These [nonpropositional strings] belong to native competence, and yet they do not fit the current key definition of human language, which involves potentially infinite creativity and production: In a word, *permutability* (p. 102)." I have been maintaining that the type of structure that significantly defies permutation is precisely the preformulation. I do not mean to demean the stunning article "Nonpropositional Speech: Neurolinguistic Studies" which is certainly the bedrock for this branch of linguistics.

Processing Time

The processing time of a syntactic structure is usually quite short, that is unless the speaker wants to be precisely exact or to take full advantage of syntax and describe an object that is not familiar to his interlocutor, such as a fan without the familiar propeller type of structure, but flat rectangular blades attached in a circle around the frame. Syntax and semantics would in all likelihood slow down until the concept were comprehended. A preformulated structure, however, would very likely seem to take far less processing time because there is normally no difficulty with confusing items. If I may make an allusion to a visual process, my point may become clear. If I look at a rather old, faded, off-white sheet of drawing paper that has been exposed to the elements, there will be many indications of this condition. A slightly dark patch next to a series of dots and other slight discolorations can be discerned, none of which have been planned or made.

My perception will, on occasion, instantly find a perfect, complete and rather interesting face or landscape or whatever. There is absolutely no slowing down of the working out of the marks on the paper trying to piece together the face or landscape: this kind of perception is virtually if not instantaneous. No time seems to have elapsed. Furthermore, it is complete down to a collar or a psychological projection. This also occurs when viewing a leafy tree from a distance. This is not, I believe, the product of my perception and none other: it seems to be common to perception in general. The relevance to preformulations is this: After the elements have been merged into a proformulation, they are apprehended with the same speed of my perception of a face on a "blank" drawing board. If these were measured, I think a similarity between preformulations and visual perception might be more evident. I realize that such anecdotes cannot be considered evidence, but I also realize that evidence can certainly develop from such observations.

Chomsky and Skinner

Now don't get me wrong. I think that syntax is simply "mahvellous" with its ability to help us systematically conceive, formulate and express subtle differences related to time and circumstance. Noam Chomsky was right in that aspect of his infamous broadside review of B.F.

Skinner's *Verbal Behavior*. But if Skinner had been a linguist (or a lawyer) and not primarily a psychologist, he could have made a formidable case for preformulations. I think that the strongest part of that case would have been an accounting for the precision that becomes possible when preformulation is added to the variation that syntax makes possible.

Code-Switching

Apparently, code-switching can be done only by two or more persons in whom fluency in at least two languages is approximately equal. For some relatively obscure reason, these persons switch languages, often in the middle of a sentence. I would like to add another vote to the argument that code-switching occurs when one of the interlocutors encounters a concept which is preformulated in the L2 but not in the L1 which he or she is speaking. Without losing a beat, the instantaneous switch is made, complete with change in accent and continuing until for some other reason another switch back to the primary language of conversation--if indeed, there is a "primary language of conversation" in that given instance.

Some related to code-switching is the encountering of a hope for something that is not possible, and for which the speaker wishes to call on a mutual awareness of 17th century English literature and does not wish to imply the naive belief that no dream is impossible: one choice in such an instance would be "dream and folly of expectation" (Browne) which captures a moderate quotient of seriousness and slight wistfulness. The choice of this preformulation instead of, say, a rosier one like "to dream the impossible dream" is made. I think that it is also another example of the great precision that preformulation makes possible.

Recursiveness

The number of sentences that can be constructed from the 40,000 lexical items we are said to have in our lexicons is virtually infinite. That infinity, however, approximately doubles if we add preformulations and their recursiveness. For example, in the following, "X" is a noun, and "V" is a verb: **X is thought to have V = John is thought to have stolen the car**. I would suggest that "is thought to have" constitutes a preformulation. "Stolen the car" does not. However, the following phrase does: **"X played a major role in Y."** Used recursively, we have the following: **X is thought to have played a major role in Y**. Filling in "X" and "Y", we have the following: **John's anger is thought to have played a major role in his getting fired**. I have no time to go into it, but this might constitute the heart of "top down language learning" of preformulations as compared to the "bottom up" constructions of syntax.

Cross-Species Preformulations

Preformulation is often thought to be far simpler than syntax. After all, our cousins the monkeys construct preformulations (as do countless other species). If there is danger from above—e.g., a flying eagle--the monkey will make warning cries to his troop. These cries will be complete with unique stress, intonation, and length—all calling attention to the danger from above. If the danger derives from below—e.g., a snake--the monkey will make a different cry. Yet the monkey is apparently incapable of deconstructing either cry and inventing syntax. Even after extensive training with sign language, monkeys can barely begin to approach the latter.

However, the slight progress made along these lines by anthropologists studying communication in primates is very interesting. It suggests that the syntax we often regard as an external mathematical property might be internal enough to have undergone evolutionary development. This would seem to be preliminary evidence concerning the evolution of syntax.

The Journal of Primate Preformulations

There also seems to be a certain amount of similarity between the **function** of the primate brain and that of the human brain. This function processes certain proto-syntactic material and certain proto-preformulaic material. *"The Journal of Primate Preformulations"* might be a good title for a publication whose parameters include, of course, many if not all primate preformulations with at least annotations related to syntactic content. The magic of novel titles and expressions and similar expressions will, I hope, direct attention to what I consider a neglected area in linguistics.

Preformulation in a Wolf Pack

Preformulations in wolves might consist of arrangements like those familiar to chess players in humans: one move is a manifestation of the configurative whole. Wolf A is directly in front of the prey. Wolves B and C are on either side of the prey, cutting off avenues of escape. Wolf D grabs the tail with his mouth. Wolves E and F make incisive strikes at the victim's flanks, which form the primary target. If the prey attempts an elusive running move, the **roles** of the members of the wolf pack instantly change and different wolves will make the necessary adjustments--yet the **pattern of attack** will remain the same. This strategy of attack is analogous to proto-preformulation. The shifts among the players are analogous to proto-syntax.

Preformulations and Lexical Items

It is, I believe, quite relevant that syntax and preformulations are instrumental in the **discovery** of relationships, as much as in the **exchange** of information concerning those discovered relationships. Concentrating on the element of discovery, we seem to find in areas such as physics and mathematics far more reliance on overt preformulation both in the holding of stipulations, proofs and procedures as well as the combination of these processes in new ways or with new data—all of which can play a part in the discovery of new theories, new problems and new solutions. In this activity, the enormous value of preformulations seems more evident than in considerations of language alone. For example, consider Farraday's Law of Induction. There are symbols but no words as such in the formulation of that law, but there is a similarity to linguistic preformulation. Both physics and linguistics depend on the unchanging and enfolding of concepts that would be impossible to hold simultaneously in consciousness. This has the familiar but remarkable effect of making it possible to process encapsulated information in mathematical powers.

As a very, very simple example, I cite the following: "Cat" enfolds the features of "fur," "paws," "tail," "purrs," "under four pounds," and "tends to be solitary." "Paws" enfolds "padded feet" and "calloused skin." "Pad" enfolds "a cushion that absorbs shock." "Shock" enfolds "sharp impact" that often causes some degree of pain. In another example, "near" enfolds several main features, including "**distance** between two or more things." If we don't have distance, we don't have "near." This process of enfolding apparently continues and multiplies ad infinitum. When we say something like "Mary had a little lamb," we are unleashing a profound storm within the synapses and dendrites of our brains. I shudder to think of what happens when we listen to the preformulated themes of Ravel's *Bolero*.

Go to Sleep—Again

Now, let's back up and consider a preformulation we referred to earlier—"go to sleep." A more straightforward expression would seem to be "*start sleeping." However, the latter is never used when the meaning is as follows: **to lose consciousness in an intentional, normal manner free from drugs or injury**. Why is "*start sleeping" never used in this context? I suggest that the reason is that **"go to sleep" <u>owns</u> this semantic territory**. "Start sleeping" might be used in reference to a subject in a laboratory that studies the process of sleep. That is, however, quite different. The semantic area occupied by "go to sleep" is staked out and will not allow "*start sleeping" into that area, any more than it will allow "go into sleep," "go sleeping," "go asleep" or any of very many close alternatives. "Fall asleep," which carries a certain lack of intention, controls an adjacent semantic area. The number of such preformulations, each of which controls a unique semantic area, is enormous in any given language. Without the variation and precision of statement and expression made possible by preformulations, syntax is vastly insufficient.

Vygotsky

Preformulations seem to behave like children or pets who resent the presence of another child or pet that is given the attention that is normally reserved for the first child or pet. What this could mean is that preformulations behave more in accord with Vygotsky's notions concerning the social nature of the child in development than like Piaget's notions of internally programmed development. Whether or not this proposition is valid, it does indicate the areas of inquiry that might open up if we consider language an agglomerative construction instead of a unified hierarchy. An hierarchical component is present, but alone, it is by no means sufficient.

The Lexical Bird

Perhaps an image is in order here. Think of a lexical item as a peacock that lives in a locked cage. The only way to unlock that cage is with a unique preformulation. If I use an approximation of that preformulation, the lock will not open. Neither can I get the lock to open by using an explanation or by attempting to discuss the constituent features of the word. The peacock with folded tail feathers represents the essential <u>en</u>folding of a large quotient of semantic information that can be <u>un</u>folded in a blinding array of features. In a 300-word stretch of discourse, the number of primary and sub-features of the various words might well number into the thousands. The conscious mind often has great difficulty in keeping track of the multiplying sub-features. It is far less disconcerting to consciously keep track of only surface syntax and surface preformulations, and to leave the labyrinthine structures to the care of the subconscious. They must, however, be properly packaged and well shipped.

The Acquisition of Preformulations

At the beginning of this paper, I said that language teaching should take under its wing and close to its heart an awareness of the curiously neglected structure we have been discussing. Once that is properly done, it will be necessary to experiment with effective ways of having students internalize preformulations. Unless the child acquires two or more languages at the same time, teachers will be up against the necessity of speeding up the acquisition of preformulations, which continue to be made at an incredible rate. At a point of high proficiency in more than one languages, the learning curves will presumably begin to coincide. It should be kept in mind, however, that if a monolingual native speaker finds refuge in the solitude of Walden Pond or monastery life, outside, a great many syntactic structures will continue to undergo transformation into preformulations as the lexicon evolves at a dizzying rate. And it is my contention that each time this happens, the new structures are shunted into a location in the brain that is different from the locations of the component lexical items. So that all of us—Native as well as Non-Native speakers-- have to strain to maintain an acceptable position vis-à-vis our ever-changing language.

There is no way that any one person can ever know at any given moment all of the preformulated structures in any language. One obvious reason for this is that there are so many discoveries constantly being made in a greater and greater number of fields and sub-disciplines. With each of these discoveries, there are necessarily new preformulations cascading in the expression of findings. Such reflections easily result in a conception of language that is amazingly dynamic. Instead of a relatively fixed system of syntax and semantics, one is forced to conceive of virtually any given language as a wild beast that continually gorges itself on— among other things—an ever-increasing number of discrete preformulations.

Yet every day, more and more students pass along from level to level and eventually do manage not to fall on their faces. That is to say, the students approximate the level of universal ignorance of emerging preformulations in the native language that native speakers speak so well—or at least think they do. Our new conception of any given language must take on lexical features that carry the notion that all speakers, native and non native, of all living languages are fellow travelers in a mysterious, mythical process, a ship whose sails are stretched to the limit by differences in syntax and by multitudes of preternatural variations in the winds of preformulation.

A Closing Statement

A last point I will attempt to make in this initial argument for a sea change in language teaching is a personal reference as to how I am attempting to make ESL students write like academicians. This is indeed a quantum leap for my students, who had not the foggiest notion of preformulations. To some degree, this particular technique involves trickery and learned deceit. I once explained what I was doing to a professor of English, not of English as a second language. He was literally shocked, mildly, of course because he was a true gentleman. But shocked he still was when I explained how I constructed a list of 100 preformulations, all taken from the Olympian heights of Academic Discourse. And this is how I did it. I started late one May by assembling a collection of textbooks and journals of chemistry, history, art, physics, biology, literature and many of the other disciplines regarded as legitimate. During the summer vacation, I read a lot of this material. When I encountered what I suspected was a preformulation, I entered it on List One. If I encountered the same structure in one or more other sources, I transferred it to List Two. I sometimes found the same structure in as many as four or even five sources. This at least seemed to be strong evidence that I was dealing with a unique variety of language that exists mainly in the 6,000+ institutions of higher education in the USA.

I arbitrarily divided the final list of 100 items into ten groups, one to be covered each week of the semester. At first, I had no idea of how I would do this. Because I myself had encountered a great many preformulations in reading and writing in this variety, I knew that in writing, I would simply browse through this store and hope I made the right choice. My students, however, had no such store. Academic writing would have to come mainly from the immediate surroundings, which consisted of the ten preformulations covered in class. They would have to develop these writing skills from the inside working their way to larger and larger spaces. Could I ask my students to study the ten items for the week and to incorporate them into their writing? I had never done this and found it to be cruel and unusual. Surprisingly enough, they were delighted to see the sentences they made. They knew very well that these sentences had a little of what was very good.

I set out to write a short piece on some aspect of Ovid's account of the tragedy of Daedalus and Icarus, which I had read to them in class. This was the reading assignment. I then prepared and copied my somewhat awkward writing and distributed it as a model. My essay was by no means memorable, but it was somewhat coherent and it was about Daedalus and Icarus. When I got the student writing a week later, I saw small leaps popping up here and there. If they can remember the sophisticated preformulations as the weeks pass, they will have acquired the ability to string more and more of these high-register preformulations together. I also asked them to be aware that they would encounter similar structures in their reading for courses in different fields. I asked them to write a few such phrases each week. Their quantum leaps in academic writing would pop up more and more in their papers as they expanded their store of academic preformulations. I find it unlikely that this particular exercise will occupy more than a very small part of a foreign language body of techniques for the college student. What I do hope occurs is that teachers and students become aware of the crucial importance of pre-formed structures and that they all work on different techniques, all with the high goal of reconstructing the yellow brick road that has fallen into serious disrepair.

Appendix

A. List of high-register preformulations from Academic Discourse. Note that in this list, "X", "Y" and "Z" are noun positions; "V" is a verb; "C" is a clause.

1. Mention should also be made of __X__.
2. __X__ has to do with __Y__.
3. Had it not been for __X__, __Y__ would have __V__.
4. In this paper, it is my goal to __V__.
5. I have tried here to show that __C__.
6. __X__ is a key element in __Y__.
7. __X__ is a legitimate field of study.
8. __X__ has more in common with __Y__ than with __Z__.

9. This will involve at least a cursory study of __X__ .
10. __X__ can also decrease efficiency.

2. Writing exercise aimed at having students internalize the above structures. The following is a model prepared by the editor of this anthology. Students were asked to write a coherent comment on the account of Daedalus and Icarus as presented in the Non-ESL textbook *Retellings: A Thematic Anthology* published by McGraw-Hill Company in New York. In order to provide a model, I executed the assignment as follows.

The Imagination of Daedalus
by Clyde Coreil

*Icarus fell into the sea, not because of tension between him and his father, Daedalus, but because of a strong wish to explore the world on his own, even if it meant ignoring his father's cautious advice. Pride of his new skill in flying **was a key element in** the boy's tragic accident. Often, youth **has to do with** assertion. That is as true today as it was in ancient Greece. Indeed, Icarus **had more in common with** a young teenager of 2010 **than with** a man of 45, either in Greece or Jersey City. **In this paper, it is my goal to** point out that neither Icarus nor his father was at fault. **This will involve at least a cursory consideration of** the reason Daedalus encouraged his son to fly. **Had it not been for** Minos, who was holding them prisoner on the island of Crete, the father **would not have** suggested the sky as a way out.*

*Today, aeronautics **is a legitimate field of study**. In Ancient Greece, it was against "the laws of nature." Nevertheless, Daedalus used his imagination to design and construct wings, not only for himself but also for Icarus. **Mention should also be made of** the fact that he wept out of deep concern for the danger he was putting his son in. Yet sadness and worry **can decrease efficiency**, so Daedalus concentrated on his task. When the wings were complete, he cautioned his son to be careful and not go too low or too high.*

I have tried here to show that although he was imaginative and even artistic,

Daedalus was also a loving father. It is ironic that although his invention of human wings was successful, it was this same genius that proved to be the occasion of his profound loss. Leaving his island prison, he found another in his son's tomb.

###

I was ready for Icarian disaster, but lo and behold, I got some rather decent pieces of writing from the students. Below is one student's execution of a similar list of ten advanced preformulations, which are again in boldface.

Parents and Aspergers Syndrome
by Sejal Shah

***This finding suggests that not only do** children with Aspergers Syndrome have a hard time dealing with it, **but** parents do too. **Little is yet known about how or why** the children became sick from Asperger's Syndrome. **Children that were said to be autistic** behaved differently. Behavior **was poised to play a major role in determining** if something was wrong* *with a child. Parents that have children with Aspergers Syndrome have different problems to worry about as opposed to those who have children that are normal. More than anything parents have to accept their children first and teach those children how to accept that they have Aspergers Syndrome. Parents **should lay to rest the fears of** children having Aspergers Syntrome. If parents don't accept it, then children will have a hard time coping with themselves and it will be harder for them to live their life as normal as they can.*

*Having Aspergers Syndrome **is thought** to make you behave differently from others, but it doesn't stop you from being human beings. **It does not follow, therefore, that** they aren't capable of living a normal life, because they are; and doing things the rest of the kids are doing. **To say this is not to deny that** it can affect the siblings of those with the disorder. **It is also worth mentioning that** you have to just have patience and train them well and make them familier to the world, which will show them that it is okay to have Aspergers Syndrome. They might not be able to control their emotions and such things, but that is what makes those kids special. **It is important to make clear that** they also have the ability to do things individually and that's how it can be proven wrong to those people that believe Aspergers Syndrome is a mental disorder. A **definitive history of** Aspergers Syndrome **remains to be written.***

#

One day near mid-term, another student came up and thanked me for telling him about preformulations. It seems that this Arabic-speaking young man from Egypt was choosing items from our total list of 100 preformulations to help him write essays for other classes. He made the interesting observation that working with the preformulations from the list actually helped him in the process of developing the body of what he wanted to express in writing. That is--or at least seems to be--the preformulations enabled him to write more and to write better about the things he was studying in other classes. Carrying this line of speculation forward, therefore, it seems possible that one ancillary effect of teaching preformulated structures is that they enable a broader acquisition of the skill of writing. I would imagine that if this is true, then we might be allowed to slice the loaf again and hypothesize that one reason for the student's feeling more comfortable is that preformulations would seem to have a depth of enfoldment that is closer to fairly sophisticated writing about theoretical matters than is often found in essays composed by students of English as a foreign language. By depth of enfoldment I mean the conceptual richness or density of a particular subject.

In any case, this anecdotal comment could provide the basis for an experiment that might yield valid data. For example, Set A and Set B of subjects would be controlled for all but one variable: one would consist of writing by students with some introductions to academic preformulations; the other would have been written by students with no such training. The study would be double blind in that neither evaluators nor subjects would be aware that training in the use of specific preformulations was in any way related to the study. The criteria for evaluation would consist of a set of, say, five rubrics each of which would contain a range of 10 levels. Of great interest would be the comparative performance--expressed in terms of numbers--of Set A and Set B. This and similar experiments would indicate if preformulations are indeed the basis of a Sea Change in language instruction or only of an arrogant tempest in a fragile teacup.

***

Endnote:

Although this is hardly the place to launch into a possible justification of a larger notion of preformulations, it would also be out of balance not to briefly note the other structures which I would suggest classifying as belonging to this relatively little explored feature which will, I hope, be studied and taken into the classroom..

- *Lexical Preformulations:* Specific words forming larger units that recur (see above).

- *Structural Preformulations:* Shapes of sentences recur. Examples: (1) To walk with Jane is what Leo loves to do. (2) Having no money, I went home. (3) Anne doesn't like to go hunting, to clean her room, and to go out with loud young men.

- *Intonational Preformulations:* (1) What? Are you crazy?

  (2) Well, he never did that to me!

- *Psychological Preformulations:* (1) Okay! I'm ready to come down now! (2) And who, may I ask, are you? (3) Who are you to tell me what to do? **Note:** Utterances that express heightened emotional states such as fear, apprehension, anxiety, challenge, dread, and terrible realization are each given their own characteristic intonational features.

- *Identificational Preformulations:* Placement of the voice—high and front, back and low, etc.—is usually indicative of the conscious or unconscious conception of what is appropriate and sought for in one's identity. ***Note:*** I once heard the familiar voice of a high city official vary from its "nasal forced resonant position"—this seemed to be his possible attempt to rise to a higher social class. For a few moments, he abandoned this apparently affected speech as he was being severely criticized by the press. His response was quite irritated if not angry. A few moments later, he regained his composure and returned to the nasal front resonant position. This phenomenon is frequently encountered in the British "Received Pronunciation," an accent that is—as far as I know—found in no native dialect of English but is singularly appropriate for formal, particularly royal functions.

Whether or not some of the above could be said to be preformed is questionable. However, stretches of speech are repeatedly influenced by them in well defined situations. This seems to be closely related to the defining characteristic of preformulations.

***

References

Browne, Sir Thomas. (1658). *Urne Buriall.* Cambridge University Press: Cambridge.

Coreil, Clyde (1992). *Fusion in Language: A Case for Supralexical Units.* New York: Dissertation, City University of New York.

Chomsky, Noam (1957). *Syntactic Structures.* The Hague: Mouton.

Dabrowska, Ewa (2004). *Language, Mind and Brain.* Washington, D.C.: Georgetown University Press.

Lewis, Michael (1993). *The State of EST and a Way Forward.* Hove, England: Language Teaching Productions.

Obler, L.K. and Gjerlow, K. (1999). *Language and the Brain.* Cambridge University Press: Cambridge.

Pawley, A. and Syder, F.H. (1980). "Two Puzzles for Linguistic Theory: Nativelike Selection and Nativelike Fluency." In J.C. Richards and R. Schmidt (eds.) *Communicative Competence.* London: Longmans.

Skinner, B.F. (1957). *Verbal Behavior.* New York: Appleton Crofts.

Van Lancker, Diana (1987). "Nonpropositional Speech: Neurolinguistic Studies." In Andrew W. Ellis, ed., *Progress in the Psychology of Language: Volume Three.* Hillsdale, New Jersey: Lawrence Erlbaum. pp. 49-108.

Yorio, Carlos (1985). "Fossilization." Draft of an unpublished paper presented at the Applied Linguistics Winter Conference in New York City.

-----. (1989) "Idiomaticity as an Indicator of Second Language Proficiency." In *Bilingualism across the Lifespan: Aspects of Acquisition, Maturity, and Loss.* K. Hytlestam and L. Obler, eds. New York: Cambridge University Press. pp. 55-72.

———————————

Bibliography

The following sources pertain to *Term Papers and Academic Writing: A Classroom Text.* Because it names several works that were not cited in this book, it is called "Bibliography." If it had been a list of all and only the publications cited, it might well have been called "Works Cited" or "References."

Andrade, Maureen S., ed. *TESL Reporter: A Forum for and by Teachers of English to Speakers of Other Languages.* Hawaii: Brigham Young University.Vol. 41, No.1. April, 2008.

"Boys to men: How Boys Develop Masculinity Through Sports." *Direct Essays.* Retrieved on 13 September 2012. www.directessays.com/viewpaper/39738.html.

Brand, Stewart (1998). "Written on the Wind." *Civilization.* Library of Congress: Washington, D.C. October/November.

Chomsky, Noam (1957). *Syntactic Structures.* The Hague: Mouton.

Coreil, Clyde. ed. (2007). *Imagination, Cognition and Language Acquisition: A Unified Approach to Theory and Practice.* Jersey City, NJ: New Jersey City University.

Coreil, Clyde, ed. (2011). *The 'X' Point in Education: Where Imagination is Lost.* Jersey City, NJ: New Jersey City University.

Gaffney, Kathleen (2003). "Unleashing Creative Competence" in *Multiple Intelligences, Howard Gardner and New Methods in College Teaching,* Clyde Coreil, ed. Jersey City, NJ: New Jersey City University.

Jeffries, Dexter (1996). "Who I Am" in *Identities: Readings from Contemporary Culture.* Ann Raimes, ed. Boston: Houghton Mifflin Co.

Mabry, Anne et al (2012). *Writing Skills Assessment Form: Research Papers.* Jersey City, NJ: New Jersey City University.

Moi, Claudia Ferradas. "Rock Music: The Literature our Students Listen To" in *The Journal of the Imagination in Language Learning and Teaching.* Clyde Coreil, ed. Jersey City: New Jersey City University. Vol II (annual), 1994.

Moore, Catriona, Judith A. Koller, Maria Kreie Arago (1994). "The Role of Art in Language Learning" in *The Journal of the Imagination in Language Learning,* Volume 2. New Jersey City University: Jersey City, NJ.

Pawley, Andrew. Personal communication, 2010.

Retellings: A Thematic Literature Anthology (2004). M.B. Clarke and A.G. Clarke, eds. Boston: McGraw-Hill.

Steinberg, Ivan (2012). *AFTerthoughts*: The AFT [American Federation of Teachers] Local 1839 Newsletter. : New Jersey: New Jersey City University. Spring/Summer.

Trimmer, Joseph F. (2006). *A Guide to MLA Documentation.* Seventh ed. Boston: Houghton Mifflin.

Turabian, Kate L., et al (2010). *Student's Guide to Writing College Papers.* Fourth ed. Chicago: Chicago University Press.

Vygotsky, Lev Semenovich (1962). *Thought and Language.* ed. and trans. by Eugenia Hanfmann and Gertrude Vakar. Chicago: Cambridge: The M.I.T. Press.

Wilkins, David A. (1976). *Notional Syllabuses.* Oxford: Oxford University Press